Mastering
Your Emotions

Mastering Your Emotions

Colin Dye

New Wine Press

New Wine Ministries
PO Box 17
Chichester
West Sussex
United Kingdom
PO19 2AW

ISBN–10: 1–903725–64–X
ISBN–13: 978–1–903725–64–1

Typeset by CRB Associates, Reepham, Norfolk
Cover design by CCD, www.ccdgroup.co.uk
Printed in Malta

Contents

Emotions:
The Signals of Your Heart

Introducing emotions

In 1959 Dorothy L. Law wrote an insightful poem regarding the effect that parental behaviour has on a child's emotional and behavioural development – both negative and positive. She said,

> If a child lives with criticism, he learns to condemn
> If a child lives with hostility, he learns to fight
> If a child lives with fear, he learns to be apprehensive
> If a child lives with pity, he learns to feel sorry for himself
> If a child lives with ridicule, he learns to be shy
> If a child lives with jealousy, he learns to feel guilt

BUT,

If a child lives with tolerance, he learns to be patient
If a child lives with encouragement, he learns to be
    confident
If a child lives with praise, he learns to be appreciative
If a child lives with acceptance, he learns to love
If a child lives with honesty, he learns what truth is
If a child lives with fairness, he learns justice
If a child lives with security, he learns to have faith in
    himself and those about him
If a child lives with friendliness, he learns the world is a
    nice place in which to live [1]

The poem accurately describes how children "learn what they
live". The environment that is set for a person in childhood plays
a major role in shaping them as an adult. Notice how in every
one of the assertions made above, *emotions* play a central part:
jealousy = guilt, acceptance = love etc. Many people's life
experience is one of growing up oppressed by negative circumstances, rather than enjoying positive input and affirmation, and
in that environment, negative emotions are bred and take root.
As those negative emotions are continually played out, they are
embedded in one's personality and do much to shape and form
the character of the adult person. The result can be a somewhat
dysfunctional person, dominated by negative emotions, who
often struggles to access positive emotions, feeling that they are
somehow "blocked" and their life is less than enriched.

   If we could only learn the secret of mastering our emotions
however, we could learn how to handle ourselves in every

situation and circumstance. Rather than be pushed around by our emotional pre-programming, it is possible to learn how to develop a healthy emotional life, so that when we experience certain environments or activities, we experience emotions appropriate to them.

I don't mean to imply that an emotionally whole person will never experience *any* negative emotions. Negative emotions are normal and at times helpful. The negative emotion of fear, for instance, triggers a reaction of self-preservation and helps us to avoid danger. It is the type of fear that helps you to run when you are in danger of being run over by a bus! This is distinct from the irrational fear which causes people to suffer from phobias. But there are many different kinds of emotion that we must learn to embrace, because an emotionally healthy person is someone who may experience the full range of human emotions without being dominated by them. You are to master your emotions – your emotions are never to master you.

Emotions are vitally important to us as human beings. They are a God-given part of our personality, providing a richness, colour and depth to our life experience that can be a source of great pleasure. But of course, things can go wrong with our emotions. Negative emotions can be alarming at times and if we are dominated by them it can lead to a miserable existence. Emotional pain is very real and can be extremely severe. Sometimes, emotional pain is even more unbearable than physical pain because there is no evident cause for it. With physical pain you can pinpoint a problem and seek the appropriate treatment, as with a wound or a broken bone, but it is vastly more difficult to pinpoint the cause of emotional pain.

Most people, to a greater or lesser degree, suffer from fear or anxiety. They experience unexplained feelings of melancholy at times, uncontrolled feelings of anger, hurt, resentment or, in extreme cases, hatred. Sometimes our emotions can be so turned in on ourselves that we are filled with feelings of dread, self-loathing, guilt and condemnation. One of the greatest obstacles to overcoming negative emotions like these is the problem of denial. We commonly ignore negative emotions because society has told us we are not supposed to feel that way. This is a double-edged problem for Christians because the Church has been effective in teaching believers that we are supposed to feel happy, blessed and full of joy all of the time; it is how we are meant to feel, they say, *because* we are Christians! Therefore, if a believer is not feeling happy and blessed, they tend to hide their negative emotions. If there is something else going on inside of us we tend to deny it, push it down and say it doesn't exist. We come to church on Sunday, we smile, we're nice to people, we tell everybody we're fine and we go home feeling as miserable as when we came. That's not reality! We need to be honest, open with our feelings, and understand that at times, even as Christians, things can go wrong with our emotions.

So far I have majored on the negative aspects of our emotions, but of course emotions can be extremely positive. As believers it is wonderful to be able to worship God with our emotions for instance – as long as we don't simply seek emotionalism in and of itself. Charismatic Christians are often castigated for being over-emotional, yet God has made us with a personality that comprises three major elements – the mind, the will and the emotions. We should live before God whole and complete in each of these dimensions, utilizing each aspect in our worship of

Him. Our thoughts should be renewed; our emotions should be in line with and reflect the spiritual realm; our choices should be in line with God's will.

General pointers on emotions

Later in this chapter we will come to a very important reason why we must become skilled in recognising and handling our emotions, but before we discuss it I want to give some general pointers that I trust will help us to have a balanced perspective on our emotions.

The difficulty of identifying and expressing emotions

It is interesting to me that, even though we live in a feeling-orientated world, many people still find it extremely difficult to identify and express their emotions. Sometimes we are not really aware of what we are feeling, or indeed the strength of the emotions that lie just under the surface of our personality. Often we have no clue as to why we are feeling what we are feeling or where these emotions originated from.

Have you ever been in a situation where you feel something strange and you don't know why? Maybe you are feeling very angry or frustrated, or perhaps you're feeling very low and you can't put your finger on why? Often it is because we are simply "out of touch" with our emotions, but deeper than that, we have no idea what it is that actually *triggers* those emotions. Fundamentally, many of us don't know how our emotions operate and so we have no means of controlling them. I hope to show you in this book how our emotions function and how we can control them. More importantly, I want to point out what

God expects us to do with our emotions so that we can enjoy all the things that He has for us.

Education is biased towards intellect and not emotion

Our education system, especially in the west, teaches us how to think, but it doesn't teach us how to feel. Education is mainly concerned with pumping the intellect full of ideas, but it does not address our emotional development at all. I imagine there are few, if any, reading this book who can say that at school they were taught to *feel*. Rather we are taught to *think*, to focus on ideas and concepts, to evaluate and process information. We are not taught to appreciate what is going on inside ourselves.

Wrong teaching about emotions

Just because you are a Christian, it doesn't mean to say that your emotions are perfectly in line with what God intended for you. Believers are just as prone as anyone to carry all kinds of emotional baggage around with them. But we must learn, with the Holy Spirit's help, to be aware of those things and ask God to deal with them.

Many Christians have been wrongly taught that emotions (or to be emotional) are usually negative. We are told to follow facts, not feelings; to do what we should, not what we feel. Although this is true and right in one sense, we must not think that God wants to deny us our emotions. He does not want us to be emotionless, soulless creatures.

We must be careful too that we don't either ignore or downplay our emotions. As we will discuss in more depth later, emotions are signals that tell us what is going on inside our hearts. If you can work out what you are feeling at any given moment, pretty soon you will have access to what's going on inside your heart and you will be able to act accordingly. Your emotions point you in the right direction. Emotions are like the "low oil" light on your car dashboard – they tell you that something is happening in the engine – the heart. The little light is not the cause of the oil being low, but the oil being low is the cause of the light! Similarly, our emotions are only indicators of what is taking place in our heart.

Cultural issues and emotions

Cultural issues have a certain role to play in how readily, or visibly, we will express our emotions, but should not prevent us from reaching emotional maturity. We may speak of the "stiff upper lip" that the British are supposed to have and there are other cultures in which public displays of emotion are frowned upon. But I cannot imagine an emotion-free existence. It would be boring, bland and colourless. God does not want to give us an operation to remove the emotional dimension of our lives so that we go around like half-baked "Dr Spocks", the half-human, half-Vulcan character from *Star Trek*!

Emotional health and its bearing on relationships

There is a heavy price to pay for unexpressed feelings that will take a toll on our relationships. When we suppress our emotions we are denying what is going on inside of us. Inevitably that affects us and it affects the way we interact with the people around us. But when we share and express our emotions with others in a God-honouring way, allowing ourselves to be vulnerable with them, it helps us to connect better with people, to resolve conflict and build genuine relationships.

It's not that relationships should be founded on emotions alone, but often the expression of our emotions will strike a chord in somebody else's heart and that's how relationships can build and develop. Emotional bonds between people are very important, so long as there are other factors in the relationship that bring stability. Feelings are important, but they must never dominate us. We must learn how to bring them under control.

Emotions: the signals of your heart

Each of us needs to develop the skill of identifying and then *owning* our emotions. All of us will, from time to time, experience the effects of negative or destructive emotions. But if we realise – like the oil light on the dashboard – that these emotions are merely *signals* to tell us something is happening in our heart – if we could arrive at that level of self-understanding – then we would be able to deal with the issues beneath the surface of our lives.

Emotions point to needs
Emotions are signals that point to needs on the inside of us. This is a vital principle to grasp and a major key to mastering your emotions. Simply put, if your needs are being met then you tend to feel good. If your needs are not being met then you tend to feel bad. It really is that simple. The state of your emotions tells you whether your needs are fulfilled or unfulfilled. If your needs are being met you will feel happy, pleased, satisfied, peaceful, but if your needs are not being met then you might experience worry, anxiety, anger, sadness.

So far, so good, but there is another important principle to grasp at this point: your feelings are not always *truthful*! In other words, although you may be feeling a certain emotion – anger perhaps – and you have to take responsibility for how you are feeling – that doesn't mean to say your emotion lines up with God's truth! We may have no right to feel angry at all, but we are experiencing that emotion because someone has hurt our feelings. So here is another important key to mastering our emotions: as followers of Jesus we need to learn how to bring our emotions in line with God's truth and God's revelation.

Let's put this another way. The message proclaimed by the world is, "If it feels good, then it is good." It is possible for a person to feel as though they are having their needs met and experience immense pleasure, whilst they are committing sin! Isn't that why people sin anyway – because they expect it in some way to satisfy their needs and desires? The Bible does not try to deny that sin is pleasurable. But it points out that the pleasures of sin are short-lived. People sin for the good feelings it brings to them, whatever they are, but it does not lead to emotional wholeness.

There are all kinds of other activities that bring good feelings for a time, such as retail therapy, for one. I know people who when they're depressed get out the plastic and go shopping. Then, after a day or so, the feel-good factor wears off. Worse still is when the credit card bill arrives. Any good feelings the shopping experience produced are definitely expelled then, to be replaced with bad or even desperate feelings. We read newspaper reports about how personal debt, especially on credit cards, is continually escalating, and more and more people are having to declare themselves bankrupt. I used to think it was only businesses that went into bankruptcy, but now ordinary people are being overwhelmed as their debts spiral out of control. Recently there was the tragic case of a man who committed suicide because he owed £70,000 on credit cards, leaving his poor wife with the bill.

All kinds of things are designed by Satan and society to make us feel good, but lead us away from God. If you feel a little low you can take a little drink, you'll feel a little better. But you can have another and another little drink until you feel so bad that you've forgotten why you had a little drink in the first place! Many in society are promoting the smoking of marijuana so that we can all "chill out". But marijuana is a mood-altering drug that, despite what people claim, can be highly dangerous. There is evidence to show that people who are predisposed to psychological problems will have such illnesses triggered by smoking marijuana.[2] Yet, despite its dangers, society is shouting, "It doesn't matter! It feels good! Come on, take a little bit!" If you are a Christian, you don't need any mood-altering drug to make you feel good about yourself and enjoy life. You need to know how to be switched on to Jesus!

Something that feels good at the time, isn't necessarily good for us and won't carry on producing feelings of wellbeing for very long. But as long we believe our needs are going to be met by a certain activity, no matter how short-lived the good feelings are, we will keep on doing it. If you believe that your needs are going to be met in a certain direction, you will be motivated to go in that direction, even if your needs are *not fully met*. Let's take the example of relationships. We live in the real world and we know that people have first, second and even third marriages. Unmarried people have multiple relationships and a number of sexual partners. Why is it then, that people still enter into multiple relationships when the likelihood is they will experience broken relationships and heartbreak? It is because they are looking for satisfaction and emotional fulfilment, and they are looking for their emotional needs to be fully met in another person – hence they are driven in that direction.

We are motivated to go in the direction where we believe our needs will be met. In other words, the direction that makes us *feel* good. Sometimes as Christians we have to admit that the feel good factor is a little elusive. I remember an evangelist who came to our church many years ago and was leading a young girl to Christ. At one point the girl informed him: "I want to keep sleeping with my boyfriend because it feels good. Your kind of Christianity that says you can't do that kind of stuff, and that makes me feel bad!" I thought the evangelist would immediately get on his high horse and lay the law down to her, but instead he said, "You know, you're right. Going God's way feels miserable at times! But it's still the right way to go."

Sometimes to go God's way doesn't feel good, but we trust God that He knows better than we do what will really satisfy our needs. Sometimes our rebellious flesh screams and protests because we want to go in an entirely different direction than where the Holy Spirit is leading us. When sin beckons our emotions yell, "Go for it!" but the Holy Spirit gently says, "Don't do it!" This is because the Holy Spirit is the Spirit of truth. God tells us the whole truth about things. He doesn't deny that there is pleasure in sin, but He wants us to know that it is shallow, short-lived, not deeply satisfying, and certainly not long-lasting. When you continually give in to your feelings then you create huge problems for yourself.

Where do emotions come from?

Emotions are not self-generating

At the root of our emotions lie our *thoughts, values and intentions* which create a desire to go in the direction we believe will meet our needs. This leads us on to discuss where emotions come from. Have you ever wondered what generates emotions in you? How does it happen? Notice that emotions are *not self-generating*. That is so important for us to understand. Emotions are a *by-product* of something else. In fact, we have no direct influence on our emotions. The little oil light on the dashboard cannot turn itself on. Its lighting up is only the effect of a hidden cause. Similarly, we cannot simply press our happy button and PING! we're happy! Our joyful emotions are just a signal that an inner need has been fulfilled.

I learned the lesson that we have no direct control over our emotions many years ago as a young ballet dancer in training. I was just starting out on my professional career and there was a certain part I was called upon to play, known as the "leo solo", which requires the dancer to behave like a lion. I had the misfortune of being taught and directed by the man for whom the solo had been choreographed many years earlier. He clearly believed that nobody on God's earth could possibly dance the part as well as he had danced it. He took me through the routine over and over again. I can still hear him now, aggressively shouting out the rhythm in order to drum it into me, "Taa ta taa ta ta, ta ta..." He clapped his hands, shouted, screamed and stomped – everything he could think of doing – until eventually I performed the dance well enough to give him some small degree of satisfaction. Then, after what seemed like a tortured eternity he said to me, "Now Colin, once more with sensitivity." I couldn't believe my ears! Sensitivity? He had wrung every last ounce of sensitivity out of me and all I wanted to do at that point was get hold of him throttle him! I was so angry! That day I learned you have no direct control over your feelings. You can't stop yourself being angry; you can't prevent your emotions from spilling out. You can try to suppress them, you can deny that they exist, but it does no good. Even if you manage to control your facial expressions well, the emotion is present, simmering under the surface. It is not helpful to bury your emotions like this. When you bury your emotions you bury them alive! Sadly, many Christians have become experts at denying their negative emotions. We are very good at denial! "Angry? I'm not angry! Praise God!" Much anger is hidden behind the sugary surface of Christian saccharine sweetness: "I'm *fine* thank you! Anyway, how are *you*?" Little wonder we lose intimacy with the Holy Spirit when we don't face up to what's going on inside us. It's simply not healthy.

Emotions are produced by our perceptions
If emotions are not self-generating, then what is it that causes them to arise? We have seen that the *root* cause is our inner needs and that we experience positive emotions when our needs are being met, and negative emotions when they are not being met. But emotions are also the product of our *perceptions*. In other words, in any given circumstance our emotions will differ depending on how we perceive the situation. How we see things tends to dictate how we feel about them.

By way of an example, let's imagine that today you really need some space to yourself. You would really value some peace and quiet because you've had a busy schedule and you need some time alone to sit and think things over for a while. How will you feel then, if the phone rings every two minutes as you are trying to relax and organise your thoughts? You will probably feel pretty irritated by the constant interruptions because at that moment your need is for silence and time to yourself.

Conversely, suppose that today you feel a little bit lonely and you need some company. You would just like to chat to somebody and have some companionship. When the phone rings you are pleasantly surprised and you chat happily to your friend. In this scenario you don't see the phone call as an irritating interruption, but rather a welcomed answer to your need for company.

You see how an identical situation can evoke a completely different emotional response depending on our perception of it at the time, and whether we feel it is hindering or helping us to have our needs met. This is why our emotions are the key to understanding our needs. Once you recognise which one of your needs demands to be fulfilled, you will be able to chart your life in the right direction, so that your needs can be truly met by the Holy Spirit. This is how we learn to deal with negative emotions especially, as we will discover in a later chapter.

Emotions – the key to understanding our needs

To understand this further we need to look at the deeper issues of our hearts. Far too much "above the surface" living takes place, even in Christian circles, for people to really be aware of their needs and to therefore understand their emotional responses. We tend to wear masks with one another constantly.

We greet each other with a fixed grin: "How are you?", "Fine!" But the truth is, we are not fine. We have to learn to communicate with one another better than this, but also to look beneath the surface of our lives and examine our hearts.

Jeremiah wrote, *"The heart is deceitful above all things and desperately wicked; who can know it?"* (Jeremiah 17:9) He was pointing to the fact that we all have a tendency towards "idolatry". In other words we attempt to get our needs met through means (typically people, circumstances and material things) other than our relationship with God. It is the basic problem of the human heart.

Idolatrous goals

Have you ever wondered why, in certain situations, unwanted emotions seem to rise to the surface? It causes us to think, "Why am I thinking that? Why am I feeling that?" and it is easy be down on yourself about it. If we learn some self-understanding in these situations however, we would discover that our emotions are a reflection of our goals and beliefs – the things that are working deep inside our heart.

A goal is something that you value or desire because you believe it will meet a need in you. What I call an "idolatrous goal" is holding the belief that something or someone apart from God is going to meet your need.

We humans have a tendency to turn away from the Lord – the only One who can truly meet all our needs – and pursue things that, in and of themselves, can't satisfy us. We will find many of those same things satisfying and enjoyable (such as relationships, material possessions, position or status) *only* when

God blesses us with them Himself as they flow out of an intimate relationship with Him. For instance, everyone is looking for love and acceptance in their life and Jesus says, "Come to Me. I'm the only One who is going to love you perfectly and accept you totally, eternally." This is true, yet we persist in trying to derive love and acceptance from those around us instead of going to Jesus first. People, if we rely on them totally, are prone to love and accept us on one occasion and reject us on another. Other people can never fully meet our emotional needs, only God can.

One of the most common misconceptions that people hold is, "When I get married I will be really happy." I hope that when you meet Mr or Mrs Wonderful and you walk down the aisle with them that you will be happy. But let me tell you this: if you're not happy now, you won't be happy then. Marriage isn't going to meet that need; only God can meet that need! You enter into marriage to give of yourself to another, to love your partner knowing that God Himself meets all *your* needs. Out of the overflow of God meeting your needs you have a surplus of love to lavish on your marriage partner.

Another common misconception is, "I'll be happy when I double my salary." But the reality is, most people who double their salary eventually double their outgoings! You need only to read the numerous stories in the media to confirm that more money does not equal more happiness. I once read a story concerning a pop star who almost had a nervous breakdown because the twelfth luxury car he ordered arrived and wasn't the right shade of blue! The fact is, if you look to "things" to fulfil your needs then you can never have enough of them. Satisfaction just does not come from material possessions.

We have to learn to put our trust and value in the right things. If we value and desire the wrong things, believing they will meet our needs, then we are headed for a fall. Some people value friendship because they believe friendship will meet their need for companionship; their primary goal is to make and maintain friendships – all well and good. Others have a need for security, so they desire money or wealth, believing this will give them security. In a general human sense, some of these things are true, but not in a basic and fundamental sense. You can have all the friends in the world and still be lonely and isolated until you're in a relationship with Jesus Christ. You can have all the money in the world, but not one need of yours will be met, because the blessings that God gives can never be bought with money.

Basic human needs

There are three basic needs that are common to all human beings – at least in the emotional, personal area of our lives – that have to be met for us to feel whole. It will help us to master our emotions if we understand at a basic level what they are:

1. The need for security
2. The need for significance
3. The need for self-worth

Security
Security is the need to be safe and accepted in the presence of unconditional love and acceptance. Most people have a number of friends, but just one or two people who they deem to be their

closest or "good" friends. Your closest friend probably accepts you as you are. They often know the best and the worst about you and it doesn't matter to them. But the Bible tells us that, *"there is a friend who sticks closer than a brother"* (Proverbs 18:24) and His name is Jesus. He will never reject you; never fail you; never leave you. The great lesson of life in the Spirit is to learn to be satisfied and secure solely in Jesus, so that even if your best friend rejects you or lets you down you can still say, "Never mind, I'm secure in Christ." I'm not talking about the "positive confession" type of false security that so many believers profess! Even a parrot can learn to say, "I'm secure in Jesus!" I'm talking about something deep in your heart – a heart knowledge of our acceptance by Father God. If we are truly secure and accepted in Christ it doesn't ultimately matter what other people say about us. It can hurt, but we can deal with the hurt because we're not looking for approval from people, but rather from God. Our basic need for acceptance, unconditional love and approval is met in Him.

Significance

The need for significance is something we all have, but is particularly apparent in men. Men need their lives to have an impact, to have meaning. At our home church we have a Men's Net – a regular gathering of men in which we seek to encourage and inspire one another to godly living. When I minister in the Men's Net I don't use the same kind of vocabulary that I would if I was preaching to a group of ladies, or even a mixed congregation. Often preachers talk about the "touch" of the Holy Spirit. But men don't want to be touched! Women want to be touched; men want to be impacted!

Each one of us wants to know that we can make a difference to our world, that our being here matters. That's why so many people place their identity in their job, their achievements, indeed, even in their ministry! It is because we want others to notice our significance in the world, but only God can confer real significance upon us.

Self-worth

The third common need is that of self-worth – the need to know that we are people of infinite value and esteem. Here particularly, we genuinely need to come into the revelation and realisation that Christ is our security. He is our significance and He is also the One who ministers to our self-worth – the only One who values us unconditionally; who puts us on this planet with a purpose to make a difference; who fills us with His Spirit and gives us the gift of infinite esteem and value. We are people of infinite value in the eyes of Jesus.

Only God can truly meet your needs

The core motivations of our lives are driven by our beliefs concerning where our needs will be met. For this reason it is vital that we understand that only God can truly meet our needs. That's why God says we are to be transformed by the renewing of our minds. If we understand that the things we commonly pursue, that we think will meet our needs, are idolatrous goals that can never meet our needs – and we understand that the real needs of our heart are only met in Christ – then we will be motivated to move more and more in Christ's direction. We will passionately pursue Jesus as the sole source for all our needs.

That's why we must have a heart that hungers after God. We need to be like David who cried out, *"My soul thirsts for God, for the living God. When can I go and meet with God?"* (Psalm 42:2 NIV). We need to learn to desire God above all things. That is true repentance – to turn away at a heart level from the things that displease God and begin to have a passion and desire for Him and His ways.

Our true significance lies in doing the will of God, and real satisfaction in life is achieved by following God's plan, understanding that His way is best. If we recognise that our needs can only be met by God, we will pursue Him with all our heart and we can avoid the heartache of being let down when our idols fail us – as they surely will.

How then can we truly discover that Jesus Christ meets our needs? By discovering who we are in Him and allowing the truth of that revelation, found in God's Word, to transform us by the renewing of our minds. A good place to start this journey if you have not already done so is in Ephesians chapters 1 and 2. I worked through these chapters and noted down the many things they tell us about *who we are* in Christ. I found thirty-three points. You may find more! As an exercise, read through these chapters and meditate on what is revealed about how God views you. Ask the Holy Spirit to minister to you concerning your identity in Christ and reflect on how He can meet every one of your needs. I list the thirty-three points that I found below:

1. You are blessed with every spiritual blessing
2. Chosen before the foundation of the world
3. Holy and without blame
4. Loved by the Father

5. Predestined for a relationship with God

6. Adopted as a son of God

7. Pleasing to Jesus Christ

8. A demonstration of His praise, glory and grace

9. Accepted in the well beloved Son of God

10. Redeemed and set free

11. Forgiven

12. An inheritor of God

13. Secure in Christ

14. Enlightened with spiritual revelation, knowledge and wisdom

15. Empowered and enabled by God

16. Seated with Christ in heavenly places

17. At the right hand of the Father

18. A victorious member of the Body of Christ

19. Made alive in Christ

20. Delivered from Satan's control

21. A child of mercy

22. Saved by grace through faith

23. The Father's creative workmanship

24. Made ready for God's prepared purpose

25. Part of the commonwealth of Israel

26. Included in the covenants of promise

27. Brought near by the blood of Christ

28. A person who has immediate and permanent access to God by the Holy Spirit

29. Fellow citizens through the saints of God

30. A member of God's household

31. Built on the foundation of Christ

32. Part of the holy temple of the Lord

33. A habitation of God by the Holy Spirit.

The greatest joy you will ever have is when you truly understand that *any* and *every* need you'll ever have is met in Christ.
In that way you'll learn how to enjoy an emotionally healthy
life.

Understanding Different Kinds of Emotions

In the previous chapter we discovered that emotions are the signals of our hearts which point to underlying needs. We learned that emotions are part of our God-given personality – a gift from God – and whilst we should never deny our emotions, neither can we rely on them. Rather, God wants us to master our emotions and enjoy them. What this means, above all, is that we are not simply "feelings first" people, tossed around on the waves of our emotions, but that we are so in touch with our emotions that we can identify our underlying needs and deal with them appropriately.

Quite a few years ago I was travelling with a group of people from our church to São Paulo in Brazil. Our schedule for the trip was going to be very tight, added to which we had travelled overnight to get to our hotel and were really exhausted. The very next morning I bounded out of bed, ready to seize the day, bent over to pick something up, and tore a muscle in my back. I was doubled up in agony and I knew that I had injured myself quite seriously. I could barely stand upright and the only position in which the pain was bearable was when I was flat on my back!

Visions went through my mind of what would happen. Was I going to have to be carried on a stretcher into meetings where I was planning to pray for the sick? Should I tell my hosts I have had an extraordinary encounter with God and am permanently laid out under the power of the Holy Spirit?! I had just one clear day with nothing planned before I was due to begin an exhausting programme of teaching seminars and conference speaking. I would be on my feet for several hours every day. All I could do was trust God for my healing, believing that He would touch me and give me the power to get through it.

With this sorry scene as the backdrop, what happened next was that a delegation from another church – not my hosts – turned up to greet me and told me, "Oh, Pastor Colin, you promised you would also come and preach for us – and today is the day!"

Horrified, I responded, "I'm going to say several things to you, but I'm afraid they all begin and end with, 'no'! First of all, I can't stand up, I'm in such pain. Secondly, this is the only free day I have to rest, pray and prepare for the rest of the week. And lastly, I already have plans for today." I told them I wanted to go to pray and seek God's face on Prayer Mountain just outside of São Paulo.

"OK," my new friends said, "we will take you to Prayer Mountain and we will have a great time up there – only at least stop by the church first."

"No, no," I said, "I know what you're trying to do! You're still trying to get me to come to the church and preach, but you must understand that my back is so sore I can't even stand up today and this is the only rest day I have. I want to seek God, I want to pray. I cannot preach for you tonight."

With a resigned look the delegation seemed to accept my protests and said, "OK, never mind. We will pick you up later and take you to Prayer Mountain."

Of course, I believed them, and I was happy to be going to Prayer Mountain. That evening they came for me in their car, I got in, and we drove straight from the hotel to the church! I was so mad! In fact I was absolutely furious! We arrived at the church and I sat in the car, refusing to get out.

"Come inside," one brother said to me.

"No, I'm not coming inside," I fumed.

"Please, just come and see the church," he insisted.

"I don't want to see the church. I want to go to Prayer Mountain!" I protested.

"Won't you just come and have a cup of coffee first?" the man pleaded.

Needless to say, I eventually, reluctantly and grumpily, followed. My friends took me through a door which, I was led to believe, opened onto a room where we would have coffee. As I should have known, it actually led directly into the front of the church which was full of people and a meeting was in full swing! My heart sank as I realised I had been set up. At that moment, if I was a feelings first kind of person and had had ready access to a bazooka, there wouldn't have been a person left alive in the building!

So, there I was, sitting on the front row. I was visibly in such agony that people from the congregation were getting out of their seats and coming over to pray for me. "Oh, you look in such pain," they said. "I *am* in such pain!" I responded. "Let us pray for you," they said.

I have to report that, that night, God did not touch me. But He did speak to me.

"Colin, whose ministry is this?"

Well, it's Your ministry of course Lord," I said.

"Well, since when do you decide when you will and will not minister?"

I felt so small and convicted. There was nothing for me to say except, "OK, Lord, you win!"

When the time came I got up and began preaching. The Holy Spirit came and the power of God began to fall on the people. When it came to the ministry time at the end, God prompted me to pray for healing. The first person to come to the front for prayer was a local pastor – with a chronic back condition! Guess what? The Father decided to instantly heal this man and he began immediately to jump about, praising God. I, meanwhile, was still in terrible agony. At that meeting, many sick people were instantly healed. It was amazing, and by now I was beginning to feel pretty good about the evening. Later we went up Prayer Mountain as planned and had an incredible, wonderful encounter with God.

I recount this story for two reasons. Firstly, to show that if you are a feelings first type of person you are going to live through a great many traumas in life as your feelings pull you this way and that and ambush you when you least expect it. Although I did not feel mentally or emotionally like getting up and preaching that night and could easily have justified an attitude that said, "No way, I'm going to my hotel room and that's that," I didn't follow my feelings. Thanks to the grace of God I finally heard the voice of the Holy Spirit and cooperated with what God wanted to do for others that night. If you are a person dominated by your feelings then, the fact is, you are going to miss out.

Secondly, I wanted to share the story with you in order to be open with you, the reader, about what I was *really* feeling. I wanted to level with you. This is important. If you are a person who doesn't often level with people about your feelings, then you need to start now. When you recognise and share your feelings with others, they really begin to communicate and people can connect with you more easily. I know this story will have connected with you, because I was honest about the way I felt. Plus, you can see from the story that God is able to use somebody weak, whose pain and emotions don't always line up exactly with the Word of God. What this tells us is, despite the fact we have good and bad emotions, it is possible to master them and win through in any situation.

1. Thinking, choosing, and feeling

The Bible teaches that every human being comprises three parts: spirit, soul and body. The soul is the area that biblical scholars refer to as the "centre of our thinking", the place where we process things, make choices, and express our feelings. The problem that most people have is that they mix up the order of these three functions of the soul and push their feelings to the forefront. However, if we understand that there is a proper sequence for these functions, and learn to operate differently, it will make a huge difference to our lives.

The order in which the functions of the soul were designed to operate is this: *thinking, choosing,* and then *feeling.* Remember, *feeling* should always come last. Remember, in the previous chapter, I wrote that people will choose to go in the direction that they believe will meet their needs and will experience certain feelings as a result. It begins with an idea – a belief about where your needs will be met and what you need to do to achieve it. For instance, you may see something you want to buy. You think that if you buy it, it will make you feel good, so you go for it. Once you possess the thing, whatever it may be, you will experience either good or bad feelings depending on a number of factors – especially whether buying the object actually did ultimately meet your need.

Emotions are so much a reflection of our perceptions about life – and often our perceptions are totally wrong! Imagine this situation: you've had a bit of an argument with a friend and although you are uptight about it and feel justified in blowing them out of the water, you calm down and decide that you will be gracious. You call them and get their answer phone, so you leave a message saying that you need to talk to them. The hours tick by and no response is forthcoming. "They must have heard the message by now," you think, becoming slightly irritated, and decide to call again. There is no answer again and so you leave another message, after all, you really do want to put the situation right. And you wait ... and wait ... and nothing happens!

Now the feelings of anger bubble up again. "I know what they're doing," you tell yourself. "They're still cross with me and they are determined not to make up! They think I'm the one in the wrong and they want to make me suffer a bit longer. Typical!" Maybe you leave one final, rather curt message, before saying to yourself, "That's it now. I've done my bit. If they want to be like that, they can forget about being friends."

But what if the awful, dawning realisation then comes: you got just one digit of your friend's phone number wrong and actually you have been leaving increasingly irate messages on the answer phone of a complete stranger. Has anything like that ever happened to you? Your perception was that you were being ignored, but the facts were otherwise!

This illustrates for us the complexities of being led by one's emotions and of making decisions based upon perception rather than fact. However, no one should try to suppress their emotions for fear of being led astray by them. If we have an emotion on the inside of us, one of the most important things we can do is to acknowledge its existence. How you express that emotion is a different matter, but it is important we acknowledge when we are angry, frustrated, hurt, anxious or depressed. Remember, if you try to bury your emotions then you bury them alive.

Most Christians seem to have a wrong view of emotional health. They try to express any emotion they consider to be positive and suppress any emotion they consider negative. Of course, this view is flawed, but neither should we simply vent our emotions in an uncontrolled way. Clinical psychologists will sometimes tell people to simply let all their emotions out, regardless of the consequences. I have heard of cases where counsellors have encouraged patients who have been badly hurt or abused by their fathers to get a photograph of their father and stab it to pieces with a knife or tear it to shreds. Believe it or not, one patient was told to go and urinate on their father's grave! All manner of unhelpful suggestions have been put forward in the name of clinical psychology because people believe the best way to deal with emotions is to "let it all out". But I do not believe that is a godly response, because an uncontrolled expression of emotion is:

1. Immature
2. Only reinforces the emotion
3. Doesn't address the underlying need and therefore does not get to the root of the problem.

Rather than trying to deal directly with our emotions, we need to look beneath the surface and get in touch with the needs that are causing them. Behind the emotion of anger, for instance, is invariably the need for justice: people have wronged me, therefore they should be punished. When we express our anger like that we become lawmaker, policeman, prosecutor, judge and jury, all rolled into one – yet we still haven't gotten to the bottom of the problem.

Trying to curtail an emotion whilst ignoring the need is a bit like this: you are driving your car down the motorway when you notice the oil light on the dashboard come on. You don't like the fact that the light has come on because it means you'll soon have to stop, and you're in a hurry, so you grab the nearest blunt instrument and smash the little light to pieces and think that you've dealt with the problem!

You and I know that doesn't solve the problem at all, and that further down the road the engine of that car is going to blow up! The same is true for our emotions. Expressing our emotions, however we choose to do it, does not address our underlying needs. We have to look beneath the surface to discover what it is that is producing our emotional responses. Trying to deal directly with our emotions and bring them under control without considering our needs is too superficial and never works in the long term. It is a bit like saying that you don't like a particular fruit that grows on a tree in your garden, so you strip the tree of its fruit to make it go away. All that happens is the fruit keeps on growing back. We need to deal with the root, rather than the fruit.

Clues to your emotions

So how do we begin to become more aware of our emotions and to understand the different needs that are producing them? Here are some clues to the things that are going on inside you when your emotions come to the surface.

Demanding behaviour

I remember once, not so long ago, when our Bible School had scheduled me to speak to the students. Without laying blame at anyone's door, the appointment had been sandwiched between several other commitments and the end result was that I was on an extremely tight schedule. I would literally have to dash in, do the teaching session, then leave immediately to get to my next appointment. I drove to the Bible School, running the gauntlet of the usual impossible London traffic, and all the time I was thinking, "OK, hopefully I will just have enough time to get upstairs, take my coat off, and sit down for a minute or two to relax and scan through my notes. I hope there's some nice coffee on the go."

Finally, I arrived, more than a little stressed, and dashed up the stairs. All that was on my mind at that moment was having a really good cup of coffee to help me de-stress and focus on the task ahead. But, as I opened the door and sniffed the air ... no coffee! One of the staff greeted me with a big smile and said, "Hello, Pastor Colin, glad you could make it." I remember replying – and I'm pretty sure that although it was a thoroughly biblical response and no one could fault my choice of words, there was something about the *tone* which hinted at the under-lying irritability and frustration – "Well, hmm. What about the coffee then?"

Immediately the innocent staff member said apologetically, "Sorry Pastor Colin, I'll put it on."

"No, you can't," I replied testily. "It takes fifteen minutes and I've got to preach in one minute!"

Clearly, there was something going on inside me. I managed to press the "pause" button and examine myself for a moment. "What's going on here?" I thought to myself. "Why do I feel so frustrated. It's ridiculous. These people have done their best for me and a glass of water will do." It was at that point that I connected with the underlying need that was actually causing my "surface" emotions. Because of my tight schedule I was under pressure. I was finding it a challenge to meet the expectations of others and I thought they should realise that and go the extra mile for me. In essence I was saying, "I work so hard. Why can't they consider my needs?"

In short, my need for respect was not being met at that point. It was nobody's fault. How could I expect the staff of the Bible School to know about the demands of my schedule? Plus, they had greeted me very warmly. As soon as I realised this it hit me: I did need to feel respected and yet they did respect me. I did work hard, but at the same time there were a lot of people who cared for me and who would do anything to make things easier for me. I began to thank God and my irritableness left – thankfully.

Disproportionate emotional response

Another clue to understanding our emotions and the needs that drive them is a disproportionate emotional response to stimuli. This sounds very technical so I will give a simple example. I once counselled a married couple who claimed that the crux of their problem was ... toothpaste! It sounds ridiculous, I know, but these people had a genuine problem. The wife would always squeeze the tube of toothpaste in the middle, whereas the husband liked to squeeze it from the bottom. Also, the husband always left off the top of the toothpaste, whereas the wife liked it to be put back on. They shared the same tube of toothpaste and so each morning and evening the scenario was something like this:

"That woman! She's been squeezing the toothpaste from the middle again!" The husband would grumble about it, brush his teeth, and then leave the top off. Then his wife would come to brush her teeth.

"That man – he's left the top off the toothpaste again!"

The wife would berate the husband: "You've left the top off the toothpaste again!"

"Yes, of course," he would reply irritably, "that's because you haven't used it yet!"

"It doesn't matter," she would snap back, "you should always put it on!"

It's not rocket science to work out that the real issue between these two people was not toothpaste. Yet, this was the issue that they talked about most when they came for counselling. Their emotional response to the toothpaste issue was way out of proportion. It's easy for us to see that in the cold light of day, but this couple couldn't! I gently suggested to them that the toothpaste thing was actually only an indication that there was another underlying cause. Indeed, we went on to discover that the real cause of these emotional outbursts was a series of unresolved issues that needed addressing honestly.

So often we are bad at addressing our feelings and instead we try to disguise them. Worse than ignoring our needs, we try to ignore the emotions themselves. Have you ever had a conversation something like this?

"Have you heard from John?"

"No, I have *not* heard from John!"

"Oh, I'm sorry. What's the matter? You sound upset."

"I'm *not* upset!"

"What's the matter with John?"

"Nothing!"

Although the person is trying hard not to give anything away – you know full well that something is wrong. Men are great at this! When trying to disguise their emotions, men are often moody and withdrawn. We are great sulkers. But women are very good at this too! Perhaps you are in another room and you can hear your wife in the kitchen. There seems to be an excessive amount of noise – pots and pans clanging and cupboard doors banging. It is a form of indirect communication:

"Hello darling, what's the matter?"

"Nothing!" (bang, crash, slam).

Well, if we behave like that when nothing is the matter, heaven help us when there is!

Your emotional investment

By contrast, and lest some readers think me sexist, it has to be said that usually a man's emotions are totally disproportionate to the event taking place. Let's take football as an example. All you have to do is to mention the name of their favourite / most hated football club and most guys will instantly erupt. It is so easy to push a man's emotional buttons. I even know some pastors, the quality of whose Sunday morning sermons depends pretty much on their team's Saturday afternoon performance!

What this tells us is that our emotions vary according to the degree of investment we put into a thing. If there is a person, situation, or circumstance we care very much about, then issues relating to them will be very emotive for us. Most readers will remember the collapse of Barings Bank in February, 1995, due to the unauthorised use of funds by one Nick Leeson. He single-handedly managed to get the bank £827 million in debt by speculating primarily on the Nikkei stock exchange. Reading about this in the newspaper, one might have responded, "Isn't that dreadful. Those poor people have lost all their money and that guy is now in a Singapore jail. Well, he deserves to be there." But now imagine the response of a person who had their life savings in Barings Bank. The first person made a low-level emotional response to the news. How will the second person react? They will probably go berserk! People have stronger emotions according to the degree of their investment.

Emotion denying behaviour

Just as the behaviour described above gives us clues to the fact that something is going on beneath the surface, there are also more negative aspects of behaviour that people engage in, rather than deal with their emotions and face their problems. Denial and blame shifting are perhaps the most prevalent, characterised by statements such as, "There's *nothing* wrong with me!" and "It's not my fault – you are *making me* angry!" In fact, we have a whole arsenal of weapons at our disposal that we use to avoid confronting our inner needs: criticising, being defensive, being aggressive. We hide behind these things instead of facing up to what is going on inside of us. But, when we pause and seek to pinpoint and deal with the need that is producing our emotions, we have taken a huge step towards mastering them.

Major groups of emotions

The spectrum of human emotions can be categorised into four major groups. It is helpful to be aware of these as you begin to identify your emotions and underlying needs.

1. *Gladness*. This includes such emotions as satisfaction, wellbeing, joy, happiness etc. As a group of emotions, these usually indicate that our needs are being met (or at least we think they are being met, because as we know, sometimes we engage in activities that only bring fleeting

pleasure). Some examples are: you pass a difficult exam and feel elated; you spend a whole day with someone you really like and discover they like you too, so you are happy and excited.

2. ***Fear.*** This includes worry, anxiety, insecurity etc. These emotions indicate that you are unsure whether or not your needs are going to be met. We could use the example of a student waiting for his/her exam results to arrive through the post. He/she has no real idea how the results will turn out and so he/she is anxious. He/she may remain that way until the results turn up and the outcome is known. Another example is a person who is trying to get to an important meeting. He/she is waiting for a bus, but the scheduled one doesn't turn up. When one finally does arrive it's full and drives straight past. Will he/she ever get to his/her appointment? The uncertainty of not knowing how things (particularly those things that are important us) will turn out produces fear and anxiety.

3. ***Anger.*** This can range from mild irritation to full-blown rage, but can also include such emotions as bitterness and resentment. Anger most often stems from frustration that in turn stems from an unmet need. Thinking back to my Brazil trip, my need was for rest and quietness, but I was being coerced in another direction. The longer the situation went on, the more frustrated I became, and ultimately angry. Whenever we sense that someone or something is blocking our needs, our response tends to be that of anger. A good example of this is the modern phenomenon of road rage. Drivers get angry when the traffic is congested making them late for a meeting, or when the driver in

front of them is not driving as quickly as they feel he/she should!

4. ***Sadness***. This group includes feeling low, melancholy, depressed etc. (I am not referring here to clinical depression). At times we just feel very low and are hard pressed to work out why. Often this is caused because we have an idealistic goal that is not realistically attainable, or simply because we are dissatisfied with our present circumstances. One young man had dreamed all of his childhood about being a pilot. As soon as he was old enough he tried to join the Royal Air Force so that he could begin to fulfil his dreams. Sadly, he was told that his eyesight was simply not good enough to be a pilot. Knowing that something we desperately want is unattainable is what produces sadness in us.

All of these emotions are signals that we can read to help us pinpoint our real needs. But once we identify our needs, what then? How do we cope with the needs that lie behind negative emotions? What we need to do more than anything else is to realign ourselves with the truth of God's Word and refocus our perceptions. Let's take the young man who wanted to be a pilot. Although he could not physically become a pilot, the truth of God's Word is that God has a specific plan for that man's life that will totally and utterly fulfil him. Although his expectations were not met and that caused him to be depressed, the truth about him according to God tells a different story. The young man needs to realise this and put his hope and trust in God, believing for Him to bring about his destiny. As far as his emotions go, he needs to refocus them so that he no longer views life from a negative perspective.

When I was desperate for a coffee and feeling irritable, I dealt with my emotions by acknowledging what was really going on inside me. I was judging others for not being aware of, and meeting, my needs, thinking they were not giving me due consideration. I allowed myself a moment of compassion – yes, I was very busy helping others – but reminded myself that others did care for me and actually my response was out of order.

When you begin to realign yourself with the truth and refocus your perceptions, you have taken an important step forward in mastering your emotions. I'm not pretending it is an easy thing to do, but it is possible. If you're feeling anxious about something you can look at your situation and identify what it is you're uncertain about. Even this insight begins to give you the grace and the strength to handle the emotion as you put your need into proper perspective.

Developing your emotional vocabulary

The well known American psychologist, Rollo May, talks about how people need to have a good "emotional vocabulary", meaning that we need to become much better at identifying, describing, and owning our emotions. Men are particularly bad at vocalising their emotions, perhaps because many men think that to be emotional is to be weak. Women are much better at expressing their emotions. Rollo May says, "An (emotionally) mature person becomes able to differentiate different feelings that they are experiencing into as many nuances, strong and passionate experiences, or delicate and sensitive ones, as in the different passages of music in a symphony."

Many of us, however, may feel like our ability to identify our emotions is more akin to the limited notes one can produce from a bugle! To help you begin to expand your emotional vocabulary, I have listed below numerous different nuances of the four major emotion groups.[3] Read these through a few times and begin to draw on them to more accurately describe your emotions. Notice that in each category there are levels of emotions ranging from extreme to mild forms.

- *Gladness*. Ecstatic, pleased, elated, happy, high, cheerful, delighted, confident, strong, contented, enchanted, calm, powerful, affectionate.
- *Fear*. Petrified, terrified, deeply shocked, horrified, panicky, frozen, anxious, insecure, nervous, shaky, cautious, unsure, muddled, confused, lost, apprehensive, threatened, vulnerable, scared.
- *Anger*. Disgusted, furious, bitter, seething, miffed, provoked, sore, annoyed, fed up, exasperated, frustrated.
- *Sadness*. Depressed, defeated, devastated, empty, worthless, hopeless, crushed, battered, guilty, gloomy, discouraged, unhappy, low, bruised, disappointed, hurt, ashamed, upset.

In the next chapter we will look at what it really means to walk in emotional freedom.

Walking in Emotional Freedom

God has given us a colourful palette of human emotions to draw from in order to add richness and depth to what would otherwise be a bland, insipid existence. Jesus showed us by example that it is possible to be holy and human at the same time! The Bible narrative shows that Jesus was sometimes angered by people's sin and hardness of heart and we also see Him moved with compassion and tenderness at the plight of those who are lost and misguided; He even said in the garden at Gethsemane, "My soul is troubled, even to the point of death." If Jesus could express His emotions in this way without sinning, then it is possible for us to do the same. Living life to the full includes the freedom to express the full range of human emotions.

However, it is important for us to come to the place where our emotions are entirely at the disposal of the Holy Spirit. This might sound excessively spiritual on first reading, but what I mean is this: in the ordinary things of life – family, relationships, all the things that occupy us – we can express our emotions freely, but we are not to be "feelings first" people who are *controlled* by our emotions. Instead, our emotions are to be surrendered to the Holy Spirit so that they enhance, rather than hinder, our enjoyment of life. One of the hallmarks of a mature person who has mastered their emotions is that they know how to walk in emotional freedom – fully expressing their feelings, but never being dominated by them, especially by negative emotions.

Even emotionally whole people, however, will experience negative emotions some of the time and indeed some negative emotions are necessary. The emotion of fear, for instance, is essential for helping us to avoid danger. Fear is what causes the surge of adrenalin that makes us to jump out of the way when a bus is heading straight for us. Sometimes the emotion of anger is necessary to generate a drive and passion in us – a righteous anger or indignation which rises up in us and gives us a determination to come against the devil and his schemes.

Clearly these "negative" emotions are right and proper in their context. But all of us, as fallen human beings, also have emotions that have become broken and fragmented through the ups and downs of life and we need healing from the damaging effects of negative emotions that have not originated from a valid source. We all need to grow into emotional maturity, but what does that actually look like? And what steps can we take to put ourselves on the road to emotional freedom? I believe there are four important steps we must all take: to assume responsibility for our own emotions, to refuse a blame mentality, to find healing for our damaged emotions and, importantly, to renew our minds.

1. Taking responsibility for your own emotions

This is perhaps the pivotal principle in finding emotional wholeness and is also easier than it sounds. Many people spend a lifetime blaming others for the way they feel. "If it wasn't for you," they say, "I wouldn't be feeling this way." We have a natural tendency towards blame-shifting – it is ingrained in us from an early age – but our situation is not helped by the fact that popular culture is constantly drip feeding us the idea that others are to blame for the way we feel. The lyrics of the 2006 hit by Embrace say,

> "I tried to fight the feeling, the feeling took me down. I struggled and I lost the day you knocked me out ... You should never fight your feelings, when your very bones believe them. You should never fight your feelings, you have to follow nature's law."[4]

The unspoken thought behind these words is that we are somehow disconnected from our emotions and that they control us, rather than us controlling them. Other songs have bluntly stated, "You make me feel so good," or conversely, "You make me feel so bad"! But how can another person *make* you feel anything? Is there anyone so manipulative that they have the power to *make* you feel what they want you to, whenever they choose to?

No, the truth is that our emotions are never caused by anyone or anything else. Our emotions are only generated by us. Other people, situations and circumstances can only ever be the *stimulus* for what we feel – in other words, they contribute to the environment in which our feelings rise to the surface – but they are never the root cause. To find the root of our emotions we have to look deeper within ourselves.

This is why it is so important to learn to look beneath the surface of many of our negative emotions and identify the unmet needs that cause them. Then we can begin to take responsibility for them. If we are feeling angry, then it is *our* anger we are experiencing, not somebody else's ("You are making me angry" is a familiar cry). Our emotions are ours and nobody else's. They are generated by us, belong to us and we must own them. No one else can make us feel anything.

Some readers may beg to differ at this point and insist that other people can be the direct cause of our emotions. I will give an example that seems to sympathise with their view, but the plain fact is, on close analysis, even in this situation we have a choice regarding our emotional reaction.

Suppose someone walks up to you and, unprovoked, slaps you across the face. How do you feel? One could argue that this person is the direct cause of your resulting feelings. But are they? Aside from the physical pain you are bound to feel, your emotions will vary depending on who has struck you and why. Even that information is enough to tell us that the emotions triggered in us are not simply caused by others. You may, for instance, feel shame and embarrassment if the person who hit you was a lady whom you have treated very badly. Perhaps you deserved the slap! On the other hand, you may feel angered by the injustice of the situation if you were struck by a complete stranger for no apparent reason. In that situation you would be angry and upset because you have been violated, and rightly so.

None of this takes away from the fact that the emotions are ours to deal with. Our responsibility kicks in when we realise that it is entirely our choice how we handle them. Jesus once said, "If somebody strikes you on the cheek, offer them the other one." That takes a level of self-control which initially may seem beyond most of us, but Jesus was teaching us that while we are not responsible for the hurt someone else deliberately causes us, we are responsible for how we handle the pain.

Taking the analogy further, I would suggest that the emotions you would experience in this situation depend very much on how you perceive what has happened to you. Here are three different reactions based upon three different perceptions:

(a) If you perceive that the person who hit you had no good reason to do so then you will be angry and want them to be "punished" for their actions. You may even want to hit back.

(b) If, on the other hand, you perceive that the person's act against you is an expression of their pain (because "hurt people hurt people"), then you may feel very differently about what has happened. You may feel ashamed if you were the person who caused pain to them, provoking them to lash out. Or, if you know that the person has suffered terrible abuse from others in the past and this is causing their behaviour, you may feel compassion for them and want to help. This is what I believe Jesus was feeling for us when He died on the cross, uttering the words, "Father, forgive them, for they know not what they do." Jesus could see beyond the act of rejection and violence as humanity crucified the Son of God, and He extended incredible compassion to a lost humanity He was dying to save. Jesus saw that our actions were an expression of our complete and utter lack of understanding of who He was. It sounds almost as if He is pleading our case before the Father.

(c) If you perceive the action that has hurt you as taking away the opportunity to have your needs met, then you will experience negative emotions of hopelessness. For example, perhaps your assailant was a girl whom you really wanted to form a serious relationship with, hoping she would meet your needs for affirmation and self-worth, but you had a row and it ended in disaster with the girl slapping your face and the relationship being terminated. Any person who is looking to have their needs met by another person outside of God will be vulnerable to hurt and the influence of negative emotions.

When bad things happen to us in life and spark negative emotions, we generally respond in one of two ways. Firstly, we can respond by turning inwards and blaming ourselves. In other words, we deem ourselves "worthy" to be feeling bad because we tell ourselves we deserve it. This happens when we have a lack of self-esteem, in itself an issue that needs addressing. More commonly, under the pressure of what we perceive people are doing to us, we respond by defending ourselves or by launching a counter-attack. Some people will even launch a pre-emptive strike if they even think someone is going to say anything negative towards them. "Do unto others before they can do unto you" is their philosophy! A gross distortion of Jesus' command to "Do unto others as you would have them do unto you."

Both these ways of responding are negative, fruitless and totally unproductive. Why? Because they both divert our attention away from the real root of the problem. We expend all our energy trying to sort everybody else out, when really the problem is in us. We need to own our emotions and deal with them.

Reacting with either blame-shifting or judgmentalism, whether it is directed inwardly to ourselves or outwardly to others, is always negative and damaging. Looking to the cause of our emotions is never about blame. God wants us to see through the smokescreen of blame, as He does, and begin to realise the power He can give us to master our emotions. He wants to bring us out of sinful behaviour and into emotional wholeness. We begin this journey when we acknowledge that our emotions are ours and ours alone.

2. Refuse a blame mentality

Walking in emotional freedom then, has to do with accepting responsibility for our own emotions without being down on ourselves and without blaming others. In order to do this we must to refuse to live with a "blame mentality". Unfortunately, our society promotes a culture of blame. We always want to know who is at fault when something doesn't work right; we tend to want to know who, rather than what, has gone wrong and why; the media takes pleasure in exalting celebrities, but delights even more in shooting them down.

If you work for a company that operates a blame culture then you already know that it can be a living hell. When something goes wrong people are more interested in finding a scapegoat than putting the problem right. Good management promotes a "no blame" culture. We should be more interested in finding out what is wrong and fixing it than identifying culprits and punishing them.

Looking for someone or something to blame ignores the problem. To return again to the analogy of a car – imagine you are driving down the motorway when your car begins chugging and eventually grinds to a halt. You open the bonnet to see what might be wrong and see that a component has worked its way loose. Maybe a spark plug has managed to pop out and the engine is not firing properly. Blame shifting is like shouting at the spark plug at the top of your voice, "I've warned you before not to do this! How dare you come out of your socket! Now my car isn't working properly and it's all because of you!"

If we react like this, putting aside the fact that people would rightly think us mad, we will unleash a torrent of emotions and probably get incredibly stressed, and yet we won't affect the situation one iota – our problem remains. In fact, the spark plug is not even listening to us – like most people who we want to blame! When you blame shift, the likelihood is, the person you are trying to blame is ignoring you. What is needed is to put the spark plug back into place and suddenly things will be OK again!

A "no blame" mentality will come from a deep understanding of ourselves. Nine tenths of the issue of mastering our emotions is to do with self-awareness. There are three things that we need to do in order to help ourselves to stop blame shifting:

(a) ***Understand that you are a person who has needs***. This is sometimes difficult for people to grasp in a society where

being described as a "needy" person has negative con-
notations. The reality is we are all needy people – *very* needy
people. Understand yourself and go easy on yourself – we all
have deep needs. Clustered around our basic human needs
are numbers of secondary needs. No one is so holy that they
have no needs! Understand that we react emotionally
whenever our needs are not being met.

(b) *Own your needs*. Unless you identify and take responsibility
for the needs you have which cause your emotional
reactions, you will never understand why you do certain
things. If you are looking for emotional security then you
will grab at something in order to try to fulfil your need.
Often we do this unconsciously because we are fallen
human beings with a bias away from God and an instinct
towards idolatry. If we can grasp that Jesus is everything
that we will ever need – He is our emotional security, He
meets our needs for significance and self-worth – then we
will stop looking in all the wrong places for fulfilment.
Following Jesus will provide the answer to our deepest
needs.

(c) *Accept responsibility for your own happiness*. As well as the
above we must take one step further. We have a choice to
pursue in Christ alone the fullness that can be found
nowhere else. In doing so we are accepting responsibility
for our own happiness. This is a very important principle of
living: you and I are responsible for our own happiness and
the Bible tells us that happiness is achieved through seeking
God. Jesus instructed us to seek God's kingdom first and
foremost and promised that as we do, "all these things"
(i.e. everything else we could possibly need) will be given

to us as well. If you seek after happiness you will miss it. But if you seek after God you will get Him and happiness too. Blessing and fullness come from seeking after Jesus. So often we go looking elsewhere. We look to people and relationships to meet our need for self-worth; we seek after a better job to meet our needs for security and significance. All of these things, Jesus said, are what pagans run after – not children of God! Rather we need to live with a Christ-centred focus.

We are not responsible for the happiness of others

Much emotional damage can result from the mistaken belief that one person can be responsible for the happiness of another person. Marriages end up on the rocks when people believe that their partner is responsible for making them happy. They are not. If you are unhappy then you must deal with it before God. No one else can make you happy in a lasting way except Him.

Many people grow up with the false notion that they can affect another person's happiness because of flawed parenting techniques. How many fathers have scolded their children by saying, "Look what you've done – you've upset your mother!" All this produces is guilt. The tragic thing is that the child is learning through this behaviour that his/her mother expects him/her to make her happy – that he/she somehow has a "responsibility" to do it. How about this one? Little Johnny comes home from school and has a bad school report. His parents look at it and they are not pleased. They say to their son, "It makes Mum and Dad *very sad* when you do badly at school." This is like putting a child into prison, as if his parents' happiness is dependent on school grades. The parents have effectively transferred the responsibility for their personal happiness and wellbeing onto the shoulders of a small boy! A boy who will, if the behaviour is repeated, grow up with guilt as he tries to do the impossible.

We can extend this analogy beyond parents and school grades. It applies even to many pastors and churches. I know some pastors who want to shoot themselves every Monday morning as they suffer from a regular attack of Monday morning blues. Why? Because if their congregation was on fire at the weekend, they are on fire, but if the congregation was dull and unresponsive, they feel down too. A church leader's happiness should never depend on their congregation – or vice versa! It has to depend on God who never changes!

Finding satisfaction in Jesus

One Easter, a Sunday school teacher was talking to her class and decided to get to the message of the real meaning of Easter via a talk on the Easter Bunny and Easter eggs etc. She asked her class, "What has long fluffy ears, eats carrots and jumps around like this [demonstrates hopping]?" None of the children responded so the teacher tried again: "You know – long, furry, floppy ears, a little pink nose, eats lots of carrots?" Eventually one boy puts up his hand and ventured, "Miss, I know because this is Sunday school the answer is supposed to be Jesus, but it sounds very much like a rabbit to me."

Just as the answer to most simple Sunday school questions is "Jesus", so the answer to all our questions in life is "Jesus" too. The trouble is that we didn't believe it in Sunday school and we don't believe it now! We are forever telling ourselves, "No, it can't be that simple!"

As Christians, we know, intellectually at least, that only God can truly meet all our needs. But so often we are alienated from this knowledge in the experience of our hearts and this can lead to many emotional problems. One of the great secrets of emotional wellbeing then, is to have our minds renewed so that we truly believe and know that only Jesus will meet every one of our needs – because that is the truth.

Emotional maturity is finding satisfaction by having your needs met through Jesus so that you can be a whole person who can cope with the passions and struggles of life more easily. It doesn't mean you sail through life like Dr Spock, immune to the vagaries of emotional turmoil, but it does mean that you know no matter what happens to you, your world will never cave in because your security is anchored in Jesus.

3. Find healing for your damaged emotions

There is no medicine, either available through the NHS or by private prescription, that can truly heal our damaged emotions. However, this book is not about saying that no Christian should be taking pills because if you loved Jesus enough you wouldn't be feeling depressed. The issue of emotional and physical wellbeing is far too complex for such dismissive platitudes – many of which, sadly, have originated from the pulpit. And I want to be careful to say that if you are reading this and you are being prescribed drugs by your doctor that are helping you with your psychological state, then you should consult your doctor before making any changes to taking your medication. However, in our lives we can be sure that Christ will come through for us in every respect and that includes healing for damaged emotions – provided we are not harbouring any sin that could hinder us.

Receiving forgiveness for our sins

With this in mind, healing for our damaged emotions has to begin with a degree of self-analysis and by confessing, repenting of and receiving forgiveness for any sin in our lives. Often our emotions are damaged purely by our own fault as the direct result of sinful behaviour. If we put our hands in the fire, then we are going to get burned! Very often the negative emotions we suffer are the result of our own foolishness.

Many years ago I counselled a lady who came to see me. I was a very young minister at the time. This lady was depressed. After I had listened to her I began to understand why she was feeling so depressed. If I had done half of what she had done over the space of just a single weekend, I would have been depressed too! I said to her, "Lady, you have gone out and done all these things over the weekend and you're complaining that you are feeling depressed. You better thank God you're feeling depressed. You ought to be feeling depressed!" (Remember, I was a young minister). "I'm glad you're feeling depressed," I continued. "If you came here feeling happy after this, then the Bible ain't true!"

These days I would put it a little more nicely, but the fact remains: given what this lady had done – given into lust, behaved irresponsibly towards herself and others, left her young son wandering the streets while she was living it up – it was not surprising she wasn't feeling very good about herself. The deeper question is: why was she going out and doing these things anyway? Was it sheer sin and rebellion or was it the result of her crying out to have a deep inner need met? What did this lady think she could possibly gain by doing what she was doing? The real tragedy was that this lady had wrong beliefs. She believed that the sex and drugs she had been indulging in would take away her loneliness and emptiness and make her feel better. Of course, her sin had the very opposite effect. This was the real issue we were addressing on that Monday morning counselling session.

Are we honest enough to admit that we have often experienced negative emotions, pain and sorrow, all because we have sinned? My hand is up! We all do this, but mercifully there is forgiveness and healing available in Christ. Sin does damage our emotions; it will produce in the believer feelings of sorrow, guilt, remorse, hurt and rejection – and ultimately dissatisfaction as you discover your needs are not really being met at all – but God can forgive us and heal us from the consequences of our sin. This is why dealing with and receiving forgiveness for sin is an essential part of having our emotions healed.

Releasing others who have sinned against us

As well as resolving the issue of our own sin it is so important to our emotional wellbeing that we forgive others as well. Not all of our pain is caused by our own sin. We have also been sinned against and injured by others. Jesus taught that we need to forgive those who sin against us because God knows that by not forgiving, we actually damage ourselves and are liable to go out and hurt other people as a result.

The Lord's prayer says, "Forgive us our sins as we forgive those who sin against us." Jesus explained that if we forgive others who sin against us then God will forgive us. But if we don't forgive others then God won't forgive us. It is a simple equation.

Note that this does not mean we are rejected by God if we harbour unforgiveness towards others, or somehow lose our salvation. But, it means that we lose out on fellowship with God and rob ourselves of the level of intimacy we could otherwise enjoy.

Jesus told a parable about a wicked servant who had been forgiven much, but refused to forgive others for the minor things they had done to him. Matthew 18:34–35 tells us the outcome for this man in Jesus' words:

> *"His master was angry, and delivered him to the torturers until he should pay all that was due to him. So My heavenly Father also will do to you if each of you, from his heart, does not forgive his brother his trespass."*

So often the negative, torturing emotions we experience are the direct result of us harbouring unforgiveness. But this kind of suffering is unnecessary. We need to forgive others and to do as Paul exhorts us in Ephesians 4:32:

> *"Be kind to one another, tenderhearted, forgiving one another, even as God in Christ forgave you."*

Receiving deep inner healing

When we have had our sins forgiven and have released other people from the sins they have committed against us, we can receive deep inner healing from Jesus and take a huge step towards wholeness. There is healing for our damaged emotions through the cross of Jesus. When Jesus died, He died to redeem the whole person – spirit, soul and body. On the cross He didn't

just carry our sin, He carried all the consequences of our sin too
– including the negative emotions that come as a result of sin.
Psalm 147:3 puts it like this:

> *"He heals the brokenhearted*
> *And binds up their wounds."*

Many of us, at one time, have been broken-hearted. Perhaps
people whom you trusted have let you down? Maybe parents or
friends did not come through for you when you needed them?
For many there have been situations that have been wounding:
the loss of loved ones; divorce, bringing separation and pain;
friends withdrawing and we don't understand why. You don't
have to live long on this earth to find that your heart can be
broken. But God wants to bind up our broken-heartedness and
heal our wounds. There is an anointing for the healing of
damaged emotions that flows from the cross of Christ. Isaiah
61:1, speaking of the Messiah to come, says,

> *"The Spirit of the Lord* GOD *is upon Me,*
> *Because the* LORD *has anointed Me*
> *To preach good tidings to the poor;*
> *He has sent Me to heal the brokenhearted . . ."*

God can heal you of rejection. He can heal you of a broken
heart. Isaiah goes on to say, still talking about this same
anointing,

> *"To comfort all who mourn,*
> *To console those who mourn in Zion,*

To give them beauty for ashes,
The oil of joy for mourning,
The garment of praise for the spirit of heaviness;
That they may be called trees of righteousness,
The planting of the LORD *that He may be glorified."*

(Isaiah 61:2–3)

There is no emotional damage so severe that it is beyond the healing touch of Jesus. He desires so much to make us whole because He doesn't want us to walk around in a damaged state being hurt and hurting others. For emotional hurt to be perpetuated from relationship to relationship, and even from generation to generation, does not bring glory to God. What glorifies God is when the cycle of emotional pain is broken and in the place of brokenness comes healing. What glorifies Jesus is when emotionally whole people offer forgiveness when they are sinned against, instead of judging and punishing – when we don't harbour feelings of poor self-worth just because others have mistreated us. From an emotionally whole person will flow an anointing that will be a soothing balm to others because just as "hurt people hurt people", it is true that "healed people heal people".

God's desire for us is to become peacemakers and learn how to intervene where normally we would hit back. Rather than retaliating when someone seems to be mistreating us, we offer understanding and compassion in return. When you are emotionally whole yourself you can understand where people are coming from when they are aggressive, spiteful and hurtful. You understand the unmet needs that drive such negative emotions and you can be a healer rather than a hurter!

Having self-compassion

When you are emotionally whole you will also discover a new depth of self-compassion, especially for the times when you go wrong. Whenever we sin we need to examine our hearts and try to understand the need we were trying to meet when we fell. It is too simplistic to merely say, "I'm just a terrible sinner. I'm worthless – I better repent." That is not true repentance, that is bondage! Jesus does not call you worthless, ever! He didn't think you were worthless when He stretched out His arms voluntarily to endure the cross for you. He thought you were worth every drop of His blood. Rather, the Holy Spirit can help you to come to a place of understanding. He can help a person to understand why they entered into a wrong relationship – because they wanted to find deep fulfilment – but that they were trying to fill a need only Jesus can fill. Have compassion on yourself, recognise the needs you are trying to meet when you sin and ask God for His forgiveness and help.

4. Renew your mind and redirect your passion

A large part of walking in emotional freedom has to do with our minds being renewed through correct alignment with the truth of the Word of God and so becoming transformed. In essence we have to believe that God will meet every one of our needs so that we are highly motivated to move in His direction. As long as we believe that any need can be fulfilled outside of our relationship with God our progress will be hindered.

When we renew our minds we redirect our passions. Passion is not wrong. We throw ourselves into things that we believe will fulfil us and do so with passion, but we need to be passionate towards the only One who can actually fulfil us – Jesus. The greatest joy of walking with Jesus is that He meets all our needs. That is the great secret of living life on planet earth.

The renewing of our mind begins with repentance, when we admit that we are out of line with God's Word. As we turn towards God and identify and renounce the false beliefs that underlie our sinful patterns of behaviour, then real transformation begins to take place.

Avoiding idolatrous goals

In chapter 1 I mentioned that anything which we substitute for God is an idol. When we seek after things outside of God which we believe will meet our needs, these are "idolatrous goals". To get a grip on our life and bring our emotions under control we have to destroy the idols in our life and have our minds renewed.

Jeremiah had to deal with idolatry in Judah. Because of the multiplication of idols in the nation the people had turned away from the Lord. As a result Jerusalem was taken. Jeremiah had to announce God's judgement because of the people's persistent idolatry and used an unusual visual image to describe the people's situation:

> "My people have committed two evils:
> They have forsaken Me, the fountain of living waters,
> And hewn themselves cisterns – broken cisterns that can hold
>   no water."

(Jeremiah 2:13)

A cistern was a kind of underground tank. In those days people would store water underground by digging a pit and lining it with clay. After the top was sealed off, water could be drawn from the tank when it was needed and it would be kept cool underneath the ground. However, if the clay lining cracked, the water would be polluted as earth seeped into it and it would become brown, brackish and undrinkable.

This is the picture that Jeremiah is drawing here: people have turned away from God who is the fountain of living water – in other words, He is a pure water supply, unpolluted and beautifully refreshing. Not only had the people turned away from God, but now they were embracing idols and Jeremiah likens these to broken water tanks that can't keep their water pure. All you can get to drink from them is muddy, polluted water that doesn't refresh and doesn't satisfy.

We do the same thing when we run after idolatrous goals. Why would anyone choose to do that? We do that when we cease to believe that God is ultimately the only source of supply for our needs – the source of pure, refreshing, living water.

Left to our own devices our tendency is always towards idolatry. We do it because of wrong beliefs – we don't truly believe God can meet all of our needs and so we search in other directions. This is why it is so important for us to have our minds renewed – to see that God alone will meet all of our needs without exception. When we understand and live in this truth, we have taken a great step towards wholeness and true emotional freedom.

4

Dealing With the Needs at the Root of Our Emotions

In this chapter we will explore more fully the needs at the root of our emotions. This is perhaps the central and most key message in this book, because in order to truly master our emotions we must understand how those emotions came about. When you can understand why you are feeling the way you are feeling – whether you are experiencing anger and frustration, happiness and joy, depression and sadness – then you can begin to deal with your emotions in a positive way.

Emotions are the expression of your needs

We have already noted that our unmet needs are the *cause* of our emotions. I would suggest to you that *any* emotion you might

feel has at its root, a specific need. The type of emotion you are
feeling at any given time is a big clue to the inner need you have.
Broadly speaking, experiencing positive emotions tends to
indicate that your needs are being met, whilst negative emotions
tend to indicate that your needs are not being met.

We must recognise the fact that God has made us with inbuilt
needs – our core needs being those of security, significance and
self-worth – and that His intention is that we seek fulfilment for
them in Him alone. The needs of our personality – body, soul
and spirit – are met by God alone through relationship with
Him, and in no other way.

When dealing with our emotions, we must deal with the *root*
before we deal with the *fruit*! In other words, we must address
our deep needs rather than attempting to superficially control
the symptoms of those needs – our emotional responses. Trying
to control the fruit will never get us anywhere.

This is one reason why it is so important to gather together
with other believers on a weekly basis to receive solid, biblical
teaching. When we realign ourselves with the truth of God's
Word it is good "root therapy" – it helps us to lay a firm
foundation in our lives and to be rightly motivated towards God,
living with our hearts open to Him. It provides us with a sound
basis from which we can examine our needs with the help of the
Holy Spirit.

Understanding your needs

When we begin to understand our needs better, we will be
better able to understand and regulate our emotions. This will
give us control over how we communicate with other people

and we will also be more prepared to accept responsibility for our own emotions. All of this is very positive and dignifying. As we increasingly accept responsibility for ourselves it is an indication that we are coming to maturity.

Remember that your emotions are your own. Other people's behaviour can be the stimulus for your emotions, but they are never, ever the root cause. The cause for all of our emotions comes from within us.

If the causes of our emotions lie within us, then how can we deal with them? The critical thing to understand is that the causes of our emotions are rooted mainly in our thinking and our perception regarding how our needs are being met, or not met, as the case may be.

Imagine this scenario: a young man is waiting to meet a young lady for an appointment of some sort. The girl he is waiting to meet is late. This man may experience a wide variety of different emotions depending on his needs at that moment and his *perception* of how those needs are, or are not, being met. Consider the following scenarios:

▶ *Scenario 1*

Suppose, for instance, this rendezvous is to be a date and that the young man's need at that moment is for reassurance – he wants to know that the girl likes him and cares for him. There is an awful lot going on inside of him emotionally right now because she is late. What is he going to be feeling? He is probably thinking, "Why is she late? Is she going to come? Does she not care about me?" He will likely be feeling anxious because he is unsure about whether his need for reassurance is going to be met. What he would like is for her to be on time or early and happy to see him. Then he would feel affirmed, reassured and all would be well.

▶ Scenario 2

Suppose the young man has no emotional attachment to this girl at all and rather than a date, this is some kind of business appointment. The young man is sitting at his desk working and waiting for her to turn up. Neither is it a particularly important appointment for the guy; it's a run of the mill, routine appointment and he is actually really under pressure with his work. He is using the waiting time to make some urgent phone calls and to send a few emails. How is he feeling? He is actually feeling *relieved* as he manages to "buy" some valuable extra time to do those urgent tasks. She is late, but he's not worried, he's relieved and even happy. It's a similar situation, but completely different emotions are at work.

▶ Scenario 3

Lastly, in the context of another business appointment with the young man sitting at his desk, we see yet another emotional scenario. This appointment is one of a number of half-hour slots the young man has today and it is currently running ten minutes late. His next appointment, however, has arrived twenty minutes early, meaning that while he is waiting for the girl to show up, the next person has arrived already and will be waiting around for him! How is he feeling? He is irritated and frustrated because his need at that time is for order. He wants to deal with his tasks efficiently and with precision. "Why can't people show up on time?" he tuts, "My appointment schedule is in chaos!"

Three similar scenarios – a guy waiting to meet a girl who is late – but three very different perceptions of the situation and accordingly, three very different emotional responses. Each of these different situations produced different results, not because of the external circumstances, but because of what was going on inside the person. Our internal needs dictate how we perceive a situation and our perception dictates how we then respond emotionally.

This is proof that our emotions are triggered by our inner needs, not by external factors, although external factors may stimulate them. If we can really grasp this, understand it and take responsibility for our emotions, then certain amazing things will begin to take place:

- We will be less judgemental of others
- We will be less critical of others
- We will understand that if we have negative emotions, they are because of unmet needs
- We will no longer blame others for the way we feel
- This will in turn help us to avoid the thoughts, words and actions that so easily alienate us from others
- We will be more aware of, and sympathetic to, the needs of others as we learn to hear in their harsh and critical language their real heart cry to have their needs met

Above all we will no longer express ourselves in ways that are *disconnected* from our needs. There are four ways in which we often respond to others that actually *ignore* our needs and point the blame away from ourselves. These will never help us to have our needs met.

- *Judgements* – "I'm in a bad mood because *you've* kept me waiting!"
- *Criticisms* – "You're *always* late, why can't you be punctual?"
- *Diagnoses* – "You didn't turn up on time *deliberately* because you wanted to embarrass me!"
- *Interpretations* – "I think she has kept me waiting because she doesn't really love me."

Rather than blaming others for the way we feel – which is a natural tendency we all have – we need to express our emotions more positively and more accurately. In order to do that we need to become much more aware of how our thoughts and feelings relate to one another.

What we feel and how we think

In order to begin to unravel and identify the distinctions between what we feel, how we think, and how we express ourselves to others we really have to learn a new emotional vocabulary. So many of the phrases that we readily use are extremely unhelpful in communicating to others what we are feeling. Take the examples below; the language is very familiar – we have all used such phrases at one time or another – but let's look at why they are misleading and unhelpful.

▶ *"I feel misunderstood."*

"Misunderstood" is not a feeling, it is a judgement. It indicates our assessment of another person's level of understanding of us. If, for instance, we are unsure of their attitude towards us (and so are not certain whether our need for self-worth will be met through this relationship) then we may feel anxious or perhaps annoyed, but we cannot feel misunderstood.

▶ *"I feel ignored."*
Again, "ignored" is not a feeling, it is a judgement or a perception we have about how others are treating us. What we are actually doing is interpreting the actions of others and *guessing* at what those actions might mean, instead of clearly expressing our own emotions and finding out the truth. In actual fact our self-esteem need is not being met and we are feeling hurt because we want to be included.

▶ *"I'm not happy at work, they make me feel unimportant."*
The word "unimportant" describes how we *think* other people are evaluating us, it is not an actual feeling. There are feelings associated with being treated as though you are not important, of course. But in such a situation one might feel sad or discouraged.

In this and many other situations what we really need to express is much more complex than the words we actually say are describing. In the above situation what we should express is that others are "behaving in such a way as to regard me as unimportant," but who ever talks like that? Because it is too much of a mouthful we shortcut it and say, "I feel unimportant," but in so doing we confuse our true emotions and make a mistake. We have used a shortcut in our speech, but we have effectively also made a shortcut in our evaluation of our emotions.

The moment we make a judgement, criticism, diagnosis or interpretation we are not expressing our emotions correctly.

And if we express ourselves in a misleading way it will almost certainly result in producing friction with the person we are trying to communicate with, as our "expressions" are heard as accusations. We will appear to be judging the behaviour of others as if we know their inner thoughts and intentions – and, of course, we know nothing of the sort.

Next time you are tempted to say that you "feel misunderstood", stop for a moment and think. You are about to make an unqualified evaluation based on your perception of others. Really what you are saying is, "I don't think those people understand me" and therefore your need for understanding and affirmation is not being met. Some emotions will be stirred as a result of that unmet need. You could be annoyed, anxious, disappointed etc., but your feelings are purely the result of your perception.

We can see from this that we need to significantly upgrade our emotional vocabulary if we are to express ourselves clearly. We must avoid using words that direct blame towards others and makes the assumption that they are guilty of mistreating us.

All of us have been in situations where we have wanted to express our feelings to someone else and they have "heard" something very different from that which we were trying to express. You tell them how you are feeling and their first reaction is, "Well, it's not my fault!" Typically, we then respond, "But, I never said it was your fault!"

How is it that when we share our feelings with others they so often interpret our words as being judgmental or accusatory? Why do they think we are blaming them? It is because we tend to use "shortcut" language to describe our feelings (similar to the statements above) and it is this that gives the wrong impression. How can one respond to the statement, "I feel ignored," except to say, "Well, *I'm* not ignoring you!"

What happens in such situations is that the person you are speaking to begins to feel annoyed because they perceive that *you* are misunderstanding *them*! They think you are trying to project blame onto them for something that they haven't done. Naturally, they want to defend themselves, because when you are under attack it is the most natural reaction – either that or you launch a counter-attack. The person might counter by saying, "You say you feel ignored, but don't you realise how stand-offish you can be. You're not that great at communication!"

At this point, the discussion becomes more heated and can degenerate into an argument. We often begin to use exaggerated language like, "You *always* do this ... you *never* explain yourself properly ..." etc. The reality is, statements like "always" and "never" are hardly *ever* true!

Marshall Rosenberg, a professor of clinical psychology, pioneered a means of communication he called "Nonviolent Communication". Rosenberg was renowned for his mediation skills and worked with a number of organisations from all spheres of life to help people understand one another and communicate better. As part of his efforts to educate people and develop their emotional vocabulary he complied various lists of words. The list I include below is a compilation of phrases that people typically use that are actually "interpretations" or "judgements" of other people based on perceptions – they are not and never can be feelings. It will help to read through the list and think about how often we use words like this to describe how we are feeling, when they are not feelings at all. I hope it will help you to redefine your emotional vocabulary and guide you towards expressing your emotions more accurately. Whenever you are tempted to use language like this to describe your feelings, stop and think again, because you are mis-communicating your needs.

- Abandoned
- Abused
- Attacked
- Betrayed
- Boxed-in
- Bullied
- Cheated
- Coerced
- Co-opted
- Cornered
- Diminished
- Disrupted
- Interrupted
- Intimidated
- Let down
- Manipulated
- Misunderstood
- Neglected
- Overworked
- Patronized
- Pressured
- Provoked
- Put down
- Rejected
- Taken for granted
- Threatened

- Unappreciated
- Unheard
- Unseen
- Unsupported
- Unwanted
- Used

I want to stress that I am not suggesting we should ever be in denial about things that have *actually* happened to us. Other people may have abused us; they may have abandoned us. We cannot disregard these actions. But when we make statements such as, "I feel abused", what we are really expressing is that through being abused, certain basic needs are going unmet and feelings associated with that have risen to the surface. What we must do is to separate our emotions from the situations we find ourselves in, firstly by owning our emotions, and secondly by carefully checking out the facts.

The woman at the well

To end this chapter there is a story in the New Testament that illustrates powerfully the fact that needs are at the root of our emotions and shows how people will pursue many irrelevant things rather than address their actual needs. This story also aptly illustrates the futility of pursuing "idolatrous goals" as mentioned in chapter 1.

John chapter 4 tells the story of a divine appointment a Samaritan woman had one day when she went to draw water from a well. She met Jesus and through a conversation He clearly pinpointed her needs and set about the task of saving her. It is a remarkable story.

It seems that Jesus went out of His way to be in the way when this woman showed up. His intent was to win her over. This woman had deep needs in her life which she was not addressing and we find that throughout their conversation Jesus broke through a number of barriers in order to get to the real heart of her problem.

As they speak, this woman tries to erect a number of barriers in order to prevent Jesus addressing the real issues in her life. First of all there is a religious barrier, then a racial barrier; there is a cultural barrier, a social barrier, and a personal barrier. She attempts five times to divert attention away from the real issue rather than face up to her deep needs. This is what people tend to do time and again. They are busy pursuing happiness and satisfaction in all the wrong places and are hiding behind barriers to avoid facing up to the truth about themselves.

This lady is playing hide-and-seek with Jesus, but her approach is obvious throughout the whole story. First of all she hides behind the fact that she's a woman and Jesus is a man. Then she hides behind the fact that she is a Samaritan and He is a Jew. As Jesus wants to probe deeper, she wants to create distance. She has so many protective measures in her self-defence. She even hides behind her religion and the different beliefs she has about worship.

Jesus only asked the woman for a drink, but His real intention was to show her that He alone could give her the living water she needed. He saw through her religious cover up; He saw through her defence mechanisms and He discerned what were her true needs and desires beyond her emotional response. Jesus had asked her for water, but she was the one who was truly thirsty. She was looking for true satisfaction and fulfilment in life but nothing she did provided it, least of all her religion. Jesus describes herself as someone who is worshipping "what you do not know", and yet He, the true Messiah, the answer to her needs, is standing right in front of her. Jesus cuts through all her pretence and exposes the true need of her heart. He does this by using a word of knowledge: "Go, bring your husband," He says. The woman responds, "I haven't got a husband."

"You're right," Jesus says. "You've had five and the man you're with now is not your husband."

She was astounded, not just because He knew these facts supernaturally, but because He was beginning to expose the true needs of her heart. Her whole life was summed up in those six relationships that Jesus pinpointed. We aren't told specifically why she had had a string of relationships, but the inference is quite clear: she had sought satisfaction in her life by pursuing one relationship after another, but had never found it. We can only guess that, tragically, each one of those relationships ended in disaster.

No wonder she had so many barriers. Can you imagine the hurt and dissatisfaction she had experienced? And the man she was currently with wasn't her husband. What does that tell us? Perhaps that though she had begun to understand that marriage wasn't going to solve her problems, she still believed that somehow a relationship with a man would. She was still motivated to go in the direction in which she believed her needs would be met.

Despite all her attempts to cover up, Jesus saw in her heart the real need that she was trying to fulfil. He could see that she was thirsty, not for a drink of water, but for something much, much deeper, and Jesus could offer it to her: a lasting relationship with someone she could truly trust and, ultimately, eternal life. She was looking for love and fulfilment, but had never found it in any of her relationships. She was the one who was really thirsty. No wonder Jesus said to her, "If you knew the gift of God and who it is just said to you, 'Give me a drink,' you would have asked him and he would have given you living water."

The "gift of God" to us today is the cool, fresh, satisfying water of life in the midst of a world that is predominantly a desert. Trying to find satisfaction away from God is like a man dying of thirst trying to drink the dry, dusty sands of the desert. Instead, Jesus offers us satisfying, living water. This woman, like so many of us, was bound by the natural world. She could only think in terms of the physical world and of seeking emotional satisfaction through physical means, but Jesus helped her to focus on the real answer.

In the next chapter we are going to look at why negative emotions offer us the best clues to what our unmet needs are.

Dealing with Negative Emotions

In this chapter I want to focus more closely upon the topic of negative emotions, since this is one issue that every person struggles with and would like to be free of. Negative emotions have a habit of hijacking us when we least expect it and are generally the cause of difficulty and misunderstanding in our relationships. At the end of this chapter we will look closely at what is often at the root of negative emotions – negative thinking – but first we will look at negative emotions, the ways in which we often try to deal with them, and how we can get them under control.

Different responses to negative emotions

There are really only three ways in which we can respond to negative emotions:

1. We can repress them i.e. hold them back.
2. We can suppress them i.e. push them down.
3. We can express them i.e. let them out.

These days, psychologists mostly tell people to pursue the third option. Their advice ranges from, "Just let it all out" to the even more dangerous, "If you feel like it, do it, it will make you feel a lot better." What this advice ignores is the fact that expressing ourselves in this manner will only *reinforce* our behaviour. If we shout angrily every time we feel irritated in order to "let out" our negative feelings, we will simply reinforce the negative thought and behaviour patterns which are the cause of our problems in the first place.

Essentially, each one of the above three is an inadvisable option. It is not right to repress or suppress our emotions and expressing them in an uncontrolled manner will be damaging. More often than not, Christians are guilty of suppressing their emotions because of the false notion they have that being a Christian means you are happy all the time. We think, therefore, that when we experience negative emotions that it must be wrong and is likely sin-related. But firstly, we need to learn that not all negative emotions are wrong (see below), and secondly, common sense tells us that as residents in a fallen world we will experience negative emotions from time to time as long as we live on planet earth! We cannot pretend our negative emotions do not exist. It is important that we acknowledge them, and more importantly, learn how to respond to them. First we need to remember that emotions are "bi-products". We need to focus on the unmet needs that are causing our emotions to be stirred in the first place.

Not all negative emotions are bad

It is helpful to understand that some so-called negative emotions are actually natural physiological responses that are perfectly normal and, in addition, some emotions that we might think of as being negative do have their place in a biblical context. Here are some examples:

▶ *Fear*

An appropriate level of fear in a given situation is normal and helpful to us in the right circumstances. Also known as "acute stress response", but more commonly known as "fight-or-flight" (a phrase first coined by Walter Cannon in the late 1920s), fear can get us out of danger when the need arises. In Africa one is taught to respect the snake. If you see a snake near your campsite, you don't act casually – rather the fight-or-flight response kicks in and we are able to take immediate and rapid evasive action. The sense of "fear" that is generated is an entirely appropriate response that launches the body into action.

From a technical point of view, the onset of "acute stress" such as this produces a sudden release of adrenalin and dopamine into the blood stream. As a result, the heart suddenly pumps five gallons of blood per minute instead of one and the blood vessels constrict to reroute blood flow away from the skin and organs to the brain and muscles. The liver dumps glucose into the bloodstream to produce a further surge of energy and the nostrils flare to facilitate an increased oxygen intake. Our pupils dilate for maximum visual perception and endorphins are released from the neo-cortex to increase our pain threshold. In this state we are ready to act as necessary to avoid or confront the present danger!

Fight-or-flight then, arising from naturally generated fear, is part of God's purpose for your self-preservation. In a more spiritual context we can think about the experience of Isaiah the prophet who, confronted with an open vision of the Lord, high and lifted up, His presence filling the temple, was struck with an awesome and godly fear. Suddenly aware of God's absolute holiness and his own uncleanness, Isaiah cried out in fear, his emotions set alight by God's very presence. What some would call the negative emotion of fear was translated into a "holy fear" that resulted in Isaiah coming into a much deeper fellowship with God and obedience towards Him.

▶ *Godly sorrow*

It was Jesus Himself who said, "Now is my soul troubled," illustrating the fact that sorrow is not always a negative thing, but can be purposeful. Although it wasn't necessary for Jesus, the Bible teaches that for the rest of us, godly sorrow also leads to repentance (2 Corinthians 7:10). When our own church takes people through our "encounter" course (a discipleship programme aimed at new believers), we take them on a journey that allows them to feel deep pain for the sins they have committed in the past that have offended God. It is a natural part of repentance and essential for dealing with the past and moving forward.

We don't tend to like the word "pain" – especially the thought of going through it. We are a bit like the man who visited the pharmacist saying, "Give me something, I'm in pain." The pharmacist replied saying, "What kind of pain?" to which the man responded, "The hurting kind of course!" As soon as we think about enduring any kind of pain we think of the "hurting" kind and say, "no way!" Yet, the Bible indicates that God often needs to bring us to a point of painful recognition of how we have offended Him with our sinful ways, making us realise that there are consequences linked to our sinful actions.

Conversely, there is of course another side to emotional pain – a worldly sorrow that doesn't lead to any kind of change at all – a lot of pain, but no gain. I have been to court many times (never as a defendant I might add!) to speak on behalf of people who were being convicted for a crime they committed, or to offer them some moral support. People are always very sorry when they come before the judge, but what were they sorry for? Mostly, they are not so much sorry for the crime they have committed as they are about having been found out. If you listed the ten commandments they would not be sorry for having broken any of them. They are sorry for having broken the eleventh commandment: thou shalt not get caught!

That kind of remorse does not bring about a healthy change, but there is a godly sorrow which is positive and helpful in bringing about repentance and brings us closer to God. Many people have benefited from experiencing the awesome presence of God in corporate gatherings. As God's power and presence is strongly manifest we want to cry out for mercy as His holiness overwhelms us and our sin comes into stark contrast. This leads us closer to Him and causes us to throw ourselves on His mercy. Jesus said, *"Blessed are those who mourn, for they will be comforted"* (Matthew 5:4 NIV).

▶ *Sorrow for the state of the nation*

The psalmist wrote, *"Rivers of water run down from my eyes, because men do not keep Your law"* (Psalm 119:136). It is time we put the full range of emotions back into our prayer life, our worship life, and our spiritual relationship with Jesus Christ. It is entirely legitimate to be grieved and sorrowful for the spiritual barrenness of our nation. At times we need to weep for our nation, as well as rejoicing in the goodness of God at other times. We need to be prepared to take the role of the intercessor and cry to God with mourning and weeping when our nation is far away from Him.

▶ *Anger*

The Bible tells us that on two occasions Jesus became angry, because the temple – His Father's house – was being defiled. In His righteous anger He overturned the tables of the money changers and drove them out with a whip. Yet, in His anger He did not sin.

To be angry with sin or angry with the devil is totally legitimate. The legendary evangelist Smith Wigglesworth was a man who was perpetually angry with the devil and his works – particularly sickness and disease. Often when he "saw" in the Spirit the root of a sickness he was moved to literally "punch" it out of the person – and did so on a number of occasions when he came across people with tumours in their stomachs. Of course, the people were healed in the process – and I don't recommend you try that at home unless you have the same kind of faith that Wigglesworth did!

People who knew Wigglesworth testified to how the emotion of anger was released in him whenever he came across the devil's work. Wigglesworth would not even wear a flower in his lapel. "As soon as you cut that flower," he would say, "it began to die. Nothing like death is going to touch my body!" This was the kind of extreme man that he was. But God used that in a positive way in Wigglesworth's healing ministry.

Emotional wholeness

Each of these different aspects illustrates the fact that our emotions are like a beautiful harp – with high notes and low notes – possessing a vast range of tones and timbres. The Holy Spirit wants our emotions to be surrendered to Him so that He can blow through the strings and play whatever music He wants; create whatever mood He wants us to experience. We will reach a place of emotional wholeness when we are prepared to allow the Holy Sprit this kind of access to our emotional life; when we trust Him with our emotions and let Him be in control instead of us.

An emotionally whole person can be angry (with sin and with the devil); fearful (not in a negative way, but in a positive way as a holy awe of God is experienced); and he/she can also be tender and compassionate; he/she is not trapped or ruled by his/her emotions, but is emotionally free and therefore able to live a life of fullness for God.

Conversely, when a person is not emotionally whole, a number of bi-products will result that will affect his/her quality of life and relationship with God:

▶ *Worship*

Our worship suffers when our emotions are constrained and worshipping God can become a dull and lifeless experience. I recall one worship leader stopping a meeting, looking out at a bunch of miserable, po-faced church members and saying, "How many people here have got the joy of the Lord deep down in their heart?" Everybody dutifully responded, so then the worship leader said, "OK, well now tell your face about that deep joy!" Some of us need our joy to be not quite so deep! We need to let some of it bubble up to the surface so that other people notice it.

▶ *Repentance*

If we are not emotionally whole, we can be insensitive to the Holy Spirit. Areas of our life where our emotions have effectively "shut down" are areas that we have made "off limits" to the flow of the Holy Spirit.

▶ *Feelings of guilt and condemnation*

Such feelings can block us from enjoying fulfilling relationships with other people, but can also close us up to the Lord.

▶ *Anger*

Feelings of anger can block out feelings of compassion and concern for other people's needs.

▶ *Self-centredness and an inability to empathise with others*

Emotionally damaged people tend to be very self-centred, preoccupied with themselves, and, therefore, unable to take up the vision and burden the Lord has for them. In London, for instance, there is a great need for the Church to be concerned about how we treat those who are homeless. But are we so taken up with ourselves and our own "problems" that we have no time for the thousands of desperately needy on our streets? It is difficult to be compassionate towards others when you are always looking inwards.

I want to show you two biblical examples that demonstrate the fact that we can only fully serve the Lord if our emotions are under control. We need to be emotionally whole and healed people if we are going to flow with the Holy Spirit.

▶ *Example 1* (Ezekiel 24:15–19)
In the prophetic ministry, as described in the Bible, often the prophets themselves were required to "become" the message God wanted them to deliver to the people. The prophets were sometimes required to "act out" God's message and sometimes they weren't acting – on occasion their life became a *living* example of their message to the nation. The latter was certainly true for Ezekiel. This is what happened to him:

> *"Also the word of the LORD came to me, saying, 'Son of man, behold, I take away from you the desire of your eyes with one stroke; yet you shall neither mourn nor weep, nor shall your tears run down. Sigh in silence, make no mourning for the dead; bind your turban on your head, and put your sandals on your feet; do not cover your lips, and do not eat man's bread of sorrow.' So I spoke to the people in the morning, and at evening my wife died; and the next morning I did as I was commanded. And the people said to me, 'Will you not tell us what these things signify to us, that you behave so?' "*

Ezekiel's wife died and he was forbidden to mourn for her. The people noticed his strange behaviour and asked what it meant. Then the prophetic word came explaining the calamity that was about the befall the people. It was to be so fast and furious that they would not have time to mourn for their dead; they would not be able to go through the traditional season of mourning and would instead have to suffer in silence. Ezekiel literally became a prophetic symbol of that to the nation.

My point is this: Ezekiel was so yielded to the Lord, and the Lord was so in control of his emotions, that he could obey God in that way. Despite the emotions of mourning, sorrow and suffering that he must have been feeling (and the verse here acknowledges that fact) he did not express them in a way that would otherwise have been completely normal and legitimate. They were kept under control because Ezekiel had yielded to the power of the Holy Spirit.

Ezekiel acknowledged his sorrow, but he was so under the control of the Holy Spirit that he didn't need to express it in a way that would otherwise have been legitimate if he had not been a prophetic minister being used by God at that time and in that way. Ezekiel had to be emotionally whole to have such control. Ezekiel is perhaps an extreme example, but we too need to know what it is to be emotionally whole if we are going to make ourselves fully available to be used by the Lord.

▶ *Example 2* (Mark 11:11)

Then there is the example of Jesus. In this passage we find a fascinating statement. It records an incident which occurred towards the end of Jesus' ministry and this particular occasion is the night before Jesus cleanses the temple for the second time.

Earlier in His ministry He had cleansed the temple, driving out those who were using it as a place to do their business. Imagine how angry Jesus must have been, therefore, that He was having to do it a second time. Mark 11:11 tells us this:

> *"And Jesus went into Jerusalem and into the temple. So when He had looked around at all things, as the hour was already late, He went out to Bethany with the twelve."*

The very next morning Jesus goes back to Jerusalem and that is when He overthrows the money-changers, scatters their tables and takes a whip to drive them out, saying, "You have made my Father's house, which should have been a house of prayer for all nations, into a den of thieves." Jesus expressed the righteous anger of the Lord, but notice that He had not lost His temper. If this had been a carnal reaction to the misuse of His Father's house then it surely would have occurred the previous night when He first saw the state of the temple. Jesus could easily have reacted on impulse and flipped, just like a mother does when she discovers her son's or daughter's room looks like a bomb site! But Jesus did not flip out. Rather, He surrendered His emotions to the leading of the Lord and *the next day*, He released that emotion under control.

Examples of uncontrolled emotions at work

Just as we have seen that some emotions generally thought of as negative can actually be positive in the hands of the Holy Spirit, there is, of course, a negative flip side. Raw, uncontrolled emotions will always have a damaging effect on us and on those around us. There are three main areas in which we need to work to get them under control:

▶ *Anger*

If you are uncontrolled and you are angry, then you are too angry to do any good. The wrath of man (or woman) does not work the righteousness of God. This is an especially important lesson for parents to learn. If you correct your children in anger, they will usually not hear your correction, but just your anger. The child will assume that you are only saying what you are saying because you are angry, not because you have a valid point of correction. Repeated over a long period of time the child's behaviour becomes geared towards avoiding making you angry, rather than learning and accepting the valid principles you want to impart to them in order to ensure their wellbeing.

Similarly, in adult relationships, if you don't control your anger when something has frustrated or upset you, then you will fail to communicate effectively. Rather than helping a person to realise they have offended or hurt you, showing anger towards them will only cause them to be defensive as they hear your criticism of them. This holds true whether you are confronting your children, your spouse, an employee, someone in authority, or a shop assistant. If you lose it, then you'll blow it!

If you have a righteous cause to deal with, do not work with uncontrolled anger. Instead submit your emotions to the Holy Spirit and let Him make you righteously angry, if that is what He decides the situation requires.

▶ *Fear*

Whilst the Bible promotes the fear of God as a good, positive thing, clearly there is such a thing as ungodly fear. "Do not fear" is one of Scripture's most repeated imperatives. Why? Because fear robs us of our trust in God's care and provision for us as His children. But, besides this kind of fear, the Bible also highlights another specific type of ungodly fear – the fear of man. *"The fear of man brings a snare"* says Proverbs 29:25. The "fear of man" will stop you from witnessing; stop you from standing up for what is right; so that fear has to be brought under control.

▶ *Negative, hopeless thoughts and feelings*
When you become, to your mind, too discouraged to pray; too depressed to praise God; you give up too soon, or you become resentful that God isn't helping you and coming through for you quickly enough, then your emotions are not under control. Again, I want to stress here that I am not talking about those suffering from acute mental illness resulting in uncontrolled emotions because of the root cause of the illness. The cruellest thing you can say to a clinically depressed person is: come on, shake yourself out of it ... here's a nice Bible verse, etc. We don't need Job's comforters! But we do need to have control over our emotions in everyday life.

How to deal with negative emotions

So, how do we control our emotions day to day? There are two important techniques to master:

1. Identify your emotions
When you are suffering from negative emotions, the first step to dealing with them is to be fully aware of what you are feeling. Sometimes, we are the last person to be aware of precisely what we are feeling and we often allow our emotions to hijack us:

"You're getting angry!" someone will say to us.

"No, I am NOT!" we respond irritably!

We need, therefore, to learn to ask ourselves regularly, "What am I feeling right now?" If you are unsure how to discern and distinguish your emotions precisely, then look at the list of emotions under the heading "Developing your emotional vocabulary" at the end of chapter 2 to get some help in identifying them. It is so important, especially when communicating to others, that you identify and express your emotions accurately. When you are happy you can be either "ecstatic" or you can be "pleased"; there is a significant difference between the two! Learn the vocabulary of emotions. If you can identify and describe accurately your emotions, it will help you deal with them and also communicate them to others more clearly.

I personally have found an appreciation of the arts a helpful way of connecting more strongly with my emotions. One thing I like about the arts – whether it is a painting, a poem, or a movie – is that it is a medium designed to provoke an emotional response in us. Every artist wants to make us feel something! Their expressed intention is to trigger certain emotions and elicit a response.

I don't know what your philosophy is about movie-going, but I think it is important to engage with our culture, to be involved and interact with it in order to bring about positive change. The movie *Hotel Rwanda* stirred deep emotions in many. Thank God that I can still go to a movie and feel something, even though I am a stuffy preacher! Thank goodness that there is something left in me that can cry. It is OK to be moved emotionally and men, especially, need to do this. I remember experiencing times of praise and worship in South America where most of the men were breaking down and sobbing in the presence of God. It was awesome. Thank God, I thought, that there are some healthy people who can be moved in the presence of God. He hasn't made us to be icebergs or stones! He has made us human beings with emotions. Don't be afraid of them!

2. Understand why you are feeling that way

Having identified accurately what emotion you are feeling, the second technique to learn is to understand why you are feeling that way. Here is a simple exercise to try: finish the sentence, "I am feeling x because I..." For example, "I am feeling disappointed because I..." and then try to identify the reason why. In this sentence the second "I" is a critical factor. It allows you to take ownership of your emotions and this is an essential part of getting them properly under control. The moment you substitute the word "you" for "I" you point the finger at someone else and you are no longer simply feeling, you are judging.

For instance: "I am feeling disappointed because *you* let me down" communicates that you are attacking the other person and it will inevitably result in conflict. Arguments begin when people feel they are being attacked and launch a defence or a counter-attack. However, "I feel disappointed because I..." helps you to take ownership and points back to the reason for your negative emotion.

We know that we experience negative emotions whenever our core needs are not being met. That is central to our understanding. But, to stretch our understanding a little further, I want to suggest to you that there are three further reasons why we might experience negative emotions. Let's look at each in turn:

▶ *Needs*

We all have core needs as discussed earlier in this book, so we might complete our sentence by saying...

- I am feeling disappointed because I need reassurance.
- I am feeling disappointed because I need some company and I am alone.

... and this would be a much more effective way of communicating our feelings. But beyond our core needs that are two other elements that make up our worldview – the way in which we perceive and understand the world, and how we relate to it. They are our values and our beliefs. If either of these are infringed it will result in negative emotions.

▶ *Values*

I was in a situation recently where I was participating on the board of a Christian organisation and as far as I was concerned the organisation was not behaving righteously. Because of this I was acting with a strong and robust, righteous indignation (which is very easy for a preacher to achieve!). However, I was getting nowhere fast. Eventually, I realised how wrong it was for me to communicate my sadness that *they* (my colleagues) were behaving in this way. So, at the very next meeting, I changed tack and said, "I'm feeling very disappointed because I value integrity in all our relationships and my need to see integrity upheld is not being met in this situation." As soon as I did that, immediately the whole situation turned around, simply because people no longer thought I was just accusing them, and we now had a shared problem.

▶ Beliefs

We might complete our sentence by saying, "I am feeling disappointed because I believe..." In other words, our belief system will have a bearing on whether we experience positive or negative emotions in a given situation. Where your needs are not being met, your values are not being expressed, or your beliefs are not being upheld, you will find negative emotions resulting. Your beliefs colour your perception of the world and act as a filter through which the events that happen to you are processed. You may, for instance, experience negative emotions based on your perception of a situation: "I'm feeling insecure because I'm not sure what the outcome of this situation will be." Your beliefs about the situation are affecting your emotions.

However, if we think about and communicate our emotions on all three levels we will enjoy much more success in our relationships with those around us. Whenever you expose your heart to others they are generally willing to hear you and listen, and are much more able to empathise with you. Negative emotions are difficult and painful and the temptation is to get rid of them as fast as possible, but we must be quick to take responsibility for them and to avoid dumping them on others.

The negativity of positive emotions

We have already discussed that sometimes when we are feeling good, it's bad! Just because it feels good for a moment, doesn't mean it is good. For instance,

- Going on a spending spree when actually you are in debt

- Binging on food and feeling good now, leading to guilt and depression later
- Indulging in an illicit relationship, leading to guilt and remorse over the sin

If you are feeling good it means that your needs are being met, but if they are being met by the wrong thing, the good feelings will be short lived. Sometimes we need to be willing to experience present pain for future gain. Another tool in your armoury for assessing your emotional state is to ask yourself the question, "Is this a godly need being met in a godly way?" If you can identify that, actually, your present need is an ungodly need (by which I mean such things as a lust for sexual gratification, or the need to be noticed by others arising out of pride) and can be, or is being, met in an ungodly way, it doesn't matter how good it makes you feel, it will be bad for you in the end. Feelings don't alter the fact that sin is sin and you must turn your back on such temptations – even if you feel bad in the short term by denying yourself.

Negative emotions can stem from negative thinking

The cause of negative emotions is often due to negative thinking, more than it is a result of our legitimate, unmet needs. We need to learn how to deal with wrong thinking – to recognise the inaccuracies and exaggerations that our thoughts are prone to.

We underestimate just how powerful negative thought processes can be, yet the effect which they have on our emotional wellbeing can be devastating. Scientific research on human thought patterns has revealed that we "produce" around 55,000 words per day in our heads as we think, interact with the world and process what we see and hear. An overwhelming 77% of that "thought output" is comprised of negative, self-defeating messages. So, for the average person, more than three quarters of all our thought processes are counter-productive – in other words, working against us! This has been enough for some therapists to dub this "voice" in our heads "the internal critic".[5]

Research also shows that by the time a person reaches the age of 18 they will have heard the word "no" 148,000 times. Inadvertently, we negatively program one another and reinforce the expectation that mostly we will receive a negative response from others. However, I believe that Christians should be, and can be, the most positive people on the planet!

I remember as a young pastor I used to go visiting in the country parish where I was based. There were certain people who were visited, without fail, every week. Yet, these same people spent the whole visit telling the pastor off allegedly for "never visiting" them. It wasn't a reflection of the truth, they were just trapped in negative thinking and unhelpful generalisations. They couldn't get over the thought patterns that had long been ingrained in their minds.

Let's take relationships: in recent years psychologists have carried out a detailed analysis of a number of relationships to find out why it is that, often, young couples begin their married life together happy and fulfilled, and yet later the relationship breaks down, falls apart and ends in divorce or separation. A recent study revealed that from a detailed assessment of newly-wed couples it was not possible at that early stage to tell apart those who would later separate and those who would remain happily married. It was nothing to do with how in love they said they were or how much affection they showed towards each other. Neither was it anything to do with how frequently they argued, nor the issues they argued about.

It seemed that there was no discernable difference between the couples who stayed together and the couples who divorced, until eventually the scientists discovered one very interesting factor which set them apart. The decisive factor turned out to be negative speech. Those who, early in the relationship, began to sow the seeds of negativity, eventually separated.

For example, in couples who ultimately stayed together the psychologists found that only around 5 out of every 100 comments directed at their spouse were negative ones. In other words, 95% of their communication towards one another was positive. In couples who would ultimately split up later on in life, they found that 10 out of every 100 comments were negative, meaning that 90% of their communication was positive and 10% negative. Although this may seem like a very small difference when expressed as a percentage – just 5% – this was enough to sow the seeds that would lead to serious conflict later on. In the end this negativity, although marginal, was enough to break down the relationship.

How much negativity you choose to listen to will affect how successfully, or unsuccessfully, you will control your negative thinking and therefore your negative emotions. If, for instance, you choose to spend a lot of time at work with the office gossip who is always criticising, backbiting and highlighting all the bad things in your workplace, you will be easily dragged down and tempted to adopt a similar attitude. This will affect how you work, how others perceive you, and could ultimately prevent you from getting a promotion. Negativity does not attract promotion!

Rather, we need to have a positive grasp of our environment and to concentrate on feeding our mind with positive influences. As we train our minds to focus on positive thoughts, that will lead to positive emotions, and indeed, this is what biblical wisdom recommends we do:

> *"Whatever things are true, whatever things are noble, whatever things are just, whatever things are pure, whatever things are lovely, whatever things are of good report, if there is any virtue and if there is anything praiseworthy – meditate on these things."*

> (Philippians 4:8)

In this chapter we have taken a global look at the issue of negative emotions and have begun to learn how to deal with them. In the following three chapters we will look more closely at the different negative emotions we commonly suffer from, examine the common pressure points which cause them, and, more importantly, learn how to deal with them.

6

Dealing With Fear and Anxiety

We know that our emotions are the signals that point to our deep inner needs – particularly our needs for security, significance and self-worth – and that we will be motivated to go in the direction where we believe those needs will be met. One of the key reasons why people pursue ends that ultimately will *not* satisfy them, is that they have misguided beliefs about what will meet their needs. When we hold false or ungodly beliefs about how our emotional needs will be met, we need to renew our minds.

The Bible is very clear in its command that we should be transformed by the renewing of our minds, and for good reason. When it comes to the area of our emotions – as with every area of our lives – God wants us to remove every false belief we have concerning how our needs will be met and to teach us to focus us on Jesus, the only One who can *truly* meet our every need.

In this chapter we are dealing specifically with the issues of fear and anxiety and looking at how we can renew our minds in order to bring these emotions under control. In subsequent chapters we will be looking at how to deal with anger, depression and loss of hope.

Causes of fear and anxiety

Fear and anxiety are rooted in *uncertainty*. Whenever we are uncertain that our fundamental needs will be met, fear and anxiety begin to rise up in us. Most people, for most of the time, can find a way of handling these negative emotions when they appear and manage to get on with their lives. In other words, they don't have a breakdown just because something doesn't go their way. This demonstrates a certain level of emotional maturity. However, there are times when emotions rise up in us and we find the feelings hard to shake off. At such times our emotions can seem out of proportion to the stimulus we are responding to and often we don't know exactly why our emotions are running rampant.

A simple example could be when we go into the bathroom, pick up the toothpaste and suddenly become incensed, yelling, "That man/woman has done it again! They've squeezed the toothpaste in the middle – AGAIN!" When we respond like that we know that there is something going on beneath the surface and that toothpaste is not the real issue!

Why is it that sometimes our emotions ambush us like this?

Usually, it is because we have some unresolved issue in our life. It could be a problem in a relationship that is important to us, or it could be because of some deep hurt that has not been dealt with. There could be numerous causes, but the fact is, although they are not always on the surface, unresolved problems lie dormant in us and do not simply go away. At times they manifest themselves through much pettier issues in our life, taking us by surprise. "Why am I so angry today?" we wonder, puzzled by our intense irritation over something quite trivial. The answer? We are angry because of some deeper issue that is frustrating us. Instead of dealing with it in the past, we have effectively "buried it alive" and now it is rearing its ugly head once more.

Deep negative emotions can surface suddenly like this when provoked. But we must remember, the stimulus for our emotions is never the cause. To find the cause we have to dig deeper. To return to the toothpaste example used earlier: the irritation displayed is indicative of an unresolved conflict with that person's spouse (the target of the anger) that needs to be resolved and put right. The first step to solving our emotional problems, then, is to take ownership of the way we feel and investigate the cause.

Accepting responsibility

"Ownership" is vitally important when dealing with our emotions. We have to own our emotions before we can master them. To this end, confession is a powerful weapon in the believer's armoury. Accurately verbalising our emotions to ourselves and to others, acknowledging that they are our emotions generated by us, is an important step forward. We also must face the fact that, at times, our negative emotions are purely due to our own sinful thought patterns or behaviour. These need to be owned and then "disowned" before the Lord – in other words, confessed, repented of and then forgiven.

Accepting responsibility for our emotions, however, does not mean that we have to become overloaded with a burden of guilt and shame. Rather it brings us dignity, release and hope, because by so doing we demonstrate to ourselves that we are not simply helpless victims of our emotions and that with God's help we can deal with them and find freedom.

One piece of advice I always give to people suffering emotionally is this: accept responsibility for your emotions, but please show yourself some compassion. Imagine for a moment that a young lady comes to you and begins to pour her heart out. "I'm so depressed," she says. "Why?" you ask. "Well, because I've been passed over for promotion at work several times and it always feels like I'm being held back. But, worse than that, I've been left standing at the altar twice and my relationships with men never seem to work out." Wouldn't you immediately feel compassion for that girl? "Poor girl!" you might think. "No wonder she's depressed." My question to the reader then, is this. If you could feel compassion for someone like that, why not show yourself some compassion? We tend to be very hard on ourselves when our emotions are out of sync. But, instead of punishing ourselves, we need to allow ourselves a moment of compassion and recognise that it is because our needs are not being met. We can then begin to investigate what is lacking in us at that moment. But we need not be overburdened with guilt during this process of self-examination.

Examining our negative emotions

Whenever we experience negative emotions the first step in assessing the underlying problem is to ask ourselves, "What need do I have that is being blocked, is uncertain, or is unattainable?" Here is a simple example that I hope will help you to begin to see how you can master your emotions in a given situation:

Imagine you are waiting for a bus and you are feeling anxious. Why are you anxious? Because you are on your way to a job interview. The bus that was due has not turned up at the scheduled time and now you are worrying that you will be late for your interview. Not only are you anxious, but you are increasingly irritated. The worst case scenario is, not only will you be late, but in your present agitated state you are not likely to give a good interview either.

How do you deal with this emotionally? First, identify precisely why you are anxious – in other words, what need in you is not being met. It is likely that you are anxious because your need to be accepted and affirmed by others (meeting your deep inner need for self-worth) is being threatened. Why? Because your perception of the situation is that your prospective employers won't be impressed if you turn up late for the interview (although you don't know for certain that this is the case). You are anxious because you are uncertain how things will turn out. You don't know whether or not your need for affirmation will be met, or whether you will be left feeling ashamed and embarrassed – all because of a late bus.

Second, you need to have a reality check. Tell yourself, "Actually, my life does not depend on this. God is in control of my circumstances and my future. The interviewers will understand if I am late, because it wasn't my fault and they will understand that this kind of thing can happen to anybody." At this point you bring the situation under control and refuse to be tossed about on an emotional tidal wave. You remove the uncertainty from the situation by establishing the fact that your life goal is much more than simply catching one bus. In all likelihood you will arrive for your interview only minutes later than you had planned, and the fact that you appear largely unruffled, whilst apologetic for your late arrival, could impress your interviewers. Here is someone who can function under pressure!

Rejecting wrong beliefs at root of our emotions

In the above example we can see how important it is to reject the false beliefs and negative thought patterns that generate so much of our negative emotions. The anxiety that welled up in the person at the bus stop was based purely upon their belief about how a person they had never met *might* react in a given circumstance. In other words, the thought process behind the anxiety was highly speculative! Recognising the flawed logic of our thoughts and seeking to correct them with the help of the Holy Spirit is how we renew our minds and bring our focus back onto Jesus.

Our childhood and general upbringing will cause us to have a particular worldview that will affect how we perceive a given situation, and therefore how we feel about it. For instance, you may hold the view that in order for you to be a worthwhile, fulfilled individual you need to marry and have children. Rather than being based on any kind of logic, such suppositions may be due to family influences – i.e. your parents/grandparents may often have said, "That's the way it has always been in our family" or less subtly, "When are *you* going to produce some more grandchildren?" It may be that they unconsciously affirm your siblings who have married and produced children, whilst prodding or encouraging you to do the same. All of this puts a strong expectation upon you to comply with the family norms – simply because the message has been drilled into you time and again.

The question is: will getting married and having children make you a truly fulfilled person? No, it won't. It need not be a disaster under this particular set of circumstances, but it certainly won't meet your deepest needs. As great as the institution of marriage is, here the belief that marriage is "the answer" is an ungodly belief and such a person needs to renew their mind and be released from the unrealistic and limiting mindset of their family.

Ungodly beliefs hit a person with a double whammy. Staying with the above example of pursuing marriage through family pressure: one, if you pursue that idolatrous goal you will eventually discover that it wasn't the solution it promised to be, and two, if you don't find a potential partner quickly and for a long time there is no prospect of marriage, you can easily fall into the trap of thinking: "Why aren't things coming together for me? Doesn't God love me any more?"

I am not suggesting that the need or desire to find a life partner is not valid. Of course it is. But Jesus asks us, "Am I not enough for you?" because He wants us to find contentment in Him first and foremost. Until you are fulfilled in Christ as a man or a woman, you are not ready to be fulfilled by another person in a relationship.

Let's look at another example: a guy says to himself, "In order for me to be a person of meaning and significance I need to be the boss of my own company; I want to run my own show." Three failed businesses and a bankruptcy later he is still saying, "I still want to run my own show," because that is how he believes his needs will be met. His wife may well be saying, "We need to talk, Mister. Why don't you go back to doing what you were doing before? You were happier then."

The above example is feasible because a key need for all men is to make an impact on the world – to be significant. Rather than finding significance in Christ, men will try to chalk up one achievement after another. The trouble is, after they achieve something, they then need to achieve something bigger and better. They make some money in business, but then they want to make more money. The question men need to ask themselves is: just how much is enough? Achieving things is good, but it is not the answer to our need for significance, because when we don't achieve, the good feelings stop.

What is the motivational drive of your life? Where do you believe your needs will be met? Each of us has to wage war against the idolatrous beliefs we hold and continually renew our mind. The most common things we chase after are people, power and possessions. None of them will meet our emotional needs, but making Jesus the centre of our lives will. We need, therefore, to replace those wrong beliefs at the root of our emotions with the right beliefs and to reorder our priorities. Focusing on Jesus will provide an anchor for our emotions. At times we are bound to struggle with negative emotions, but we need never feel so low that we are not thankful to God who meets all our needs. We need never feel so empty that we need to act immorally in order to have our needs met.

Exercise

To reject any idolatrous goal that is taking you away from the Lord, first of all seek to understand which of the following applies to you. Decide whether your negative emotion is one of:

- anxiety/fear – because of an uncertain goal
- anger/frustration – because of a blocked goal
- sadness/depression – because of an unattainable goal

Recognising once again that your needs can only be met by the Lord, redirect your passion towards Him and begin to seek Him with all of your heart. Trust Him that the positive emotions that result when you act in obedience to Him will follow.

Here is another exercise that will help you pinpoint and deal with the *cause* of your negative emotions:

1. Describe the negative emotions that are a problem to you.

   _____

2. Describe the negative effect they are having on you and other people.

   _____

3. Do you accept ownership and responsibility for these emotions? Yes/No

   _____

4. If yes, state why

    _____

5. If no, state why

    _____

6. Can you identify the need at the root of your emotion? Is it security? Significance? Self-worth?

    _____

7. What do you think, deep in your heart, will bring you real happiness and fulfilment in life?

    _____

8. Is it a relationship, romance, marriage? Money or possessions? Status or career?

    _____

The effects of fear and anxiety

These two closely linked emotions can be crippling, affecting not only our minds, but our physical wellbeing as well. Both have the same root – an uncertain goal. For anyone to suffer from fear and anxiety is lamentable, but for believers it is particularly tragic because it makes us so dysfunctional; it can dominate us and make us spiritually and emotionally immobile.

Michel de Montaigne said, "A man who fears suffering is already suffering from what he fears." That reminds me of the story of the man who heard that a wolf was roaming the forest near his village. Since his house was right on the edge of the forest, he was continually nervous that the wolf would show up and terrorise him. So, every night he would cautiously open his front door and peer out to see if he could see the wolf prowling around anywhere. The wolf, who was in the forest, noticed this and thought, "Stupid man. He keeps opening the door to me! He must want me to come in." One night, the man opened his door to look out and the wolf was right outside. So it was that eventually his worst fears were realised!

People who worry and are anxious are often suffering from the "Wallenda factor". Karl Wallenda was a great tightrope aerialist, who put his life at risk every time he walked the tightrope because he always refused to use any kind of safety net or harness. He performed tremendous, death-defying stunts all his life. In 1978, aged 73, Karl attempted to walk between two hotels in San Juan, Puerto Rico, on a wire stretched 37 metres above the pavement, but fell tragically to his death. His widow explained what happened: "He had never known fear all his life," she said. "He would walk up there with not a bit of fear. But something happened to him. He changed. He began to get very nervous ... worrying about this detail or that. One day when he stepped out on the wire I didn't recognise him – he was totally different." For the first time, instead of concentrating on what he was doing, he was worrying about not falling. It was an accident waiting to happen.

Worrying has been known to bring about the very things that we were worrying about in the first place. It is the same with fear. Fear can open a door. So, what is the answer, since we cannot simply "switch off" these emotions? The answer is to get to the root of the problem. We need to ask ourselves, "What uncertain goal is causing my fear/anxiety?" When you discover the answer you will be able to take a positive step to correct the problem.

Jesus put His finger right on this issue when He identified people's preoccupation with uncertainty about the future. "Why do you worry about what you will wear ... what you will eat etc.?" He said. People tend to be fearful because they don't know what tomorrow will bring. Sadly, this robs us of the pleasure of enjoying today. Jesus commanded us to change from this way of thinking. In Matthew 6:34 He says,

> *"Do not worry about tomorrow, for tomorrow will worry about its own things. Sufficient for the day is its own trouble."*

For many years I wondered what the second half of Jesus' statement really meant – especially in the Authorised Version which renders it: "Sufficient unto the day is the evil thereof"! Eventually, I came to realise that God has simply made us to be "one-day-at-a-time" people and that worry and fear are largely the result of us focusing on the wrong day. We tend to fret about things that mostly we cannot control. Most people live either too much in the past or too much in the future. But, the past has gone – you can't do anything about it – and the future hasn't happened yet, so you can't begin to deal with it.

The answer to dealing with tomorrow is to deal with today correctly. For example, if a student begins to prepare for his exams only a few days before he is due to sit them, he will be worried, and rightly so! But, if he has done his prep gradually and consistently throughout the academic year, he should not be unduly worried because he has equipped himself for the task ahead.

Similarly, we have to take responsibility for our lives and do the right thing today. With God's help we have to make good choices and then entrust our lives into God's hands. That way we will be building a tomorrow we can cope with. The ultimate antidote to fear and anxiety is trust – trusting God to meet all our needs and to help us deal with life's issues and challenges, one day at a time.

This, of course, implies that we are going God's way and putting Him first in our lives. That's why Jesus says, "Seek first the kingdom of God." To trust God means that you obey Him because you believe that going His way is what is best for you. We need to believe and understand that God's way really is best for us. Then we can confidently invest our lives in following God's direction because we know that He alone will meet all of our needs. When you obey God it is a demonstration of the fact that you are trusting Him and often this goes against your feelings. Why? Because very often to take a first step in the direction of God's will, instead of giving in to negative emotions, doesn't necessarily feel good. But in retrospect you will never, ever be disappointed that you obeyed God.

Fifteen steps to dealing with fear and anxiety

There are numerous admonitions throughout Scripture that command us not to worry or be anxious. Philippians 4:19 says,

> *"My God shall supply all your need according to His riches in glory by Christ Jesus."*

And again in Philippians 4:6–7 we read,

> *"Be anxious for nothing, but in everything by prayer and supplication, with thanksgiving, let your requests be made known to God; and the peace of God, which surpasses all understanding, will guard your hearts and minds through Christ Jesus."*

Here Paul is dealing directly with fear, anxiety and worry. Paul says, "If you commit everything in prayer to God you won't have to worry about it any more."

Charles Spurgeon said, "I could no more worry than I could go and commit murder. Both are sin in God's sight." God commands us not to worry because He wants us to trust Him to meet all our needs. The context of the above scriptures is physical need, but God is committed to meeting our emotional needs too, not just our physical needs. This must become a conviction in your life. Deciding to go God's way and trusting that He will supply dispels fear and anxiety.

As with many of the great promises of Scripture, God doesn't simply write us a blank cheque. We have our part to play as we walk in covenant with Him. We must fulfil certain conditions which will "position" us so that God can meet all our needs. Below are listed fifteen points, all based on Philippians chapter 4, which will aid us in our growth towards emotional wholeness and maturity. I want to stress that this is not a "formula" which guarantees success, but rather, shows us a lifestyle that if adhered to will produce maximum fruitfulness in our lives.

1. **Stand fast in the Lord** (v. 1). Don't allow your focus to shift away from the Lord, but pursue Him with all your heart. Keeping focused on Jesus will help you avoid deception and distraction.

2. **Walk in unity and peace with your brothers and sisters** (v. 2). The quality of our Christian character and spiritual/emotional life is related to our corporate life in the Body of Christ. Too often we think we can go it alone with no reference to others, or we behave one way in God's

presence and quite another when we are with other people. But we must aim to walk consistently before the Lord. This is why it is important to belong to a home group or cell group: they bring people close together and with that proximity comes interaction which brings confrontation, at times, and tests our character. If you fall out of relationship with somebody you open the door for anxiety to hit your life.

3. ***Rejoice in the Lord always ... knowing that He alone can meet your needs*** (v. 4). How do you "rejoice in the Lord?" What does it mean? It means to be well satisfied with God – He fills you, He meets all your needs, He is everything you need. He can come through for you like no other.

4. ***Walk in gentleness*** (v. 5). "Gentleness" here is a very technical Greek word and this verse in Philippians is the only one in the entire New Testament which uses it. It is a legal term and has the following application / meaning: imagine a landlord takes a lady to court and says to the judge, "This woman owes me rent money." The judge says, "Do you know anything about that woman and her circumstances? Last year she lost her husband, and her only son, who was earning the income for their family, has also died. She has nobody and no income." Is the landlord still legally entitled to receive his rent money from this lady? Yes, he is. But, instead of demanding his due, he says, "Though it is my legal right to take that rent, I am not going to exact my legal right. I will waive it and bless this lady." That's what this word "gentleness" means – when we exact less than our legal due out of compassion for someone else. Do you want peace in your life and to be free

of fear and anxiety? Then deal with people with biblical "gentleness". Only someone who knows that God will meet all their needs can really act this way.

5. ***Don't worry about anything*** (v. 6). Somebody has said that 85% of what we worry about never happens. Someone else said, 98% of statistics are made up on the spot! But, whether it is statistically accurate or not, most of us can testify to the fact that we have worried over things that ultimately never came to pass and in retrospect we felt a bit foolish for having spent so much emotional energy on them. Many of the things we worry about never actually happen. Someone else once said, "We would worry far less about what other people thought of us if we knew how little they thought of us in the first place!"

6. ***Learn to pray about everything*** (v. 7). This brings us into the realm of the real, supernatural power of God. Prayer brings about the supernatural release of God's power into your life. If you don't pray you are going to be a person who worries. But if you have dealt with the issues of your life before the Sovereign God, everything is different. Become a prayer-warrior not a prayer-worrier! This is not putting your head in the sand – there are those who never seem worried about anything and you wish they would be – rather, this is placing your trust in the God of the supernatural.

7. ***Cultivate a lifestyle of thanksgiving*** (v. 7). It is impossible to worry if you are giving thanks. If you were starving and someone sat you down at a table laden with food, your first reaction would not be to say, "But, I don't know where my next meal is coming from"; you would be very thankful for what was in front of you. "Thank you, Lord, I can eat

today!" would be your response. I have a pastor friend in Africa. We were in Kenya together and at every meal my friend's plate was piled higher than Mount Kenya! It didn't matter whether it was breakfast, lunch or dinner, every plate was piled high and he didn't seem to struggle to finish it either. I said to him, "Why do you pile your plate so high?" He replied, "You are with me today, but tomorrow I don't know what to eat. So today I eat for tomorrow!" I argued with him, "You can't eat for tomorrow – you can only eat for today!" But the point is: always thank God for what you have now!

8. *Let God's peace be the ruler of your heart* (v. 7). When God's peace rules your heart it keeps out anxious, negative thoughts. There is simply no room for them. If you seek God and are anxious for nothing His peace will rule and reign. The Bible uses an unusual word for the word "rule" which is "umpire". In other words, God will watch over the peace of your heart and will "referee" the match. He will penalise any illegal move that takes place on the pitch: "Offside!" The Holy Spirit will regulate your life and maintain the peace of God.

9. *Meditate on the positive, life-enriching things God has for you* (v. 8). When you put good things into your life it produces good results. Paul tells us to focus on things that are lovely, noble, virtuous, of a good report, praiseworthy etc. We need to use our imagination positively for the glory of God because what you focus your attention on will determine the direction of your life. A friend of mine used to race motorbikes. I asked him how he managed to ride at such high speeds and avoid hitting other riders. He said that

expert racers teach you that if you want to avoid something, you don't look at it! If you look at something hoping to avoid it, you will hit it, because when you are travelling at high speed you go in the direction of your eyes. So it is with our spiritual lives: if you want to avoid it, don't look at it!

10. *Learn how to live a godly, peaceful lifestyle* (v. 9). How do we do this? By imitating godly leaders and mature Christians. You should be able to look at your leaders, and mature brothers and sisters in Christ, and find strong role models and examples of how to live out your faith.

11. *Learn to be content with your circumstances* (vv. 10–12). Don't let the world's ambition or greed take hold of you. If you start living by the world's standards then you will suffer from the world's emotional pain.

12. *I can do all things through Christ who strengthens me* (v. 13). "Can't" is not a word in the Christian vocabulary! The fact that Jesus promises to strengthen us so that we can accomplish whatever challenge is set before us should give us an enormous amount of peace and confidence.

13. *Develop a lifestyle of loving generosity* (vv. 14–18) – especially towards God's work and those in need. If we expect God to supply all our needs then it is important that we remember to give also – that we remember to pay out tithes and to give offerings. Take care of others and God will certainly take care of you.

14. *Trust God to meet your every need* (v. 19). I mean *every* need: emotional, physical, financial, spiritual – every need.

15. *Learn to focus on God's glory* (v. 20). It is helpful to learn to focus on God and His glory rather than on yourself or your problems.

As a final exercise, ask yourself these three questions:

- "What do I need to stop doing in order to fulfil these conditions in my life?"
- "What do I need to continue to do?"
- "What do I need to start doing?"

Then develop a practical plan of action to bring these changes about and follow your plan every day for the next three weeks. After that time review your progress and describe the changes that have taken place. Continually pray for God to flood you with His peace.

7

Anger and Bitterness

" 'Be angry, and do not sin': do not let the sun go down on your wrath, nor give place to the devil ... Let all bitterness, wrath, anger, clamour, and evil speaking be put away from you, with all malice."
(Ephesians 4:26 – 27, 31)

In the previous chapter we looked at the closely related emotions of anxiety and fear. In this chapter we are looking at the twin emotions of anger and bitterness. We have seen that the answer to resolving negative emotions is to deal with what is going on in our hearts and this is never more important than when we tackle the issue of anger and bitterness. Anger focuses on something *outside* of ourselves as the root cause of our emotional pain. We direct our anger at whoever, or whatever, we believe to be the cause of our negative feelings. It is vital to grasp this, because at the most fundamental level, the way to deal with anger is simply to accept responsibility for what is going on inside us, rather than pointing blame elsewhere.

We know that the way to understand negative emotions is to relate them to our needs and goals. Previously we discovered that fear and anxiety result whenever we are uncertain that a particular goal we have will be met. Anger and bitterness result when a goal we have is being *blocked* for some reason. In other words, if we perceive that some obstacle is preventing us from reaching a particular goal, then frustration will result, eventually giving way to anger if the goal continues to be blocked.

All negative emotions have an effect on us, but anger can be particularly debilitating. Someone once described anger as an "asset that is more damaging to the vessel that contains it, than the one upon whom it is poured." Have you noticed that? So often we direct our anger at others in the hope that we can make them "sorry for what they did" to us, but the result is that we feel even more churned up and damaged than we were to begin with. There is a well-known saying, "Don't get mad, get even." But such a statement presupposes that it is right and proper to punish others for the things they do to us which we judge to be "wrong". In fact, when we pour out our anger and frustration on somebody else, we become the law-maker, arresting officer, prosecution, judge, jury and jailer all rolled into one! In reality, we are in no position to make such judgements about others and venting our anger on them will further alienate them from us, rather than solve any problem.

The seriousness and danger of anger

You don't just have to take my word for it that anger is detrimental to your wellbeing. A vast body of medical research is available to back up the claim. Listen to the words of both the medical establishment and leading counsellors:

> "At some point in their lives between 5.4 percent and 7.3 percent of US adults qualify for a diagnosis of intermittent explosive disorder (IED) [*i.e. uncontrolled outbursts of anger*] ... between 11.5 million and 16 million people respectively ... IED features tirades, grossly disproportionate to the triggering circumstances ... the expression of rage elicits a sense of relief, followed by remorse for the incident. [The] majority of [such] incidents targeted spouses or children, with potentially harmful effects on their emotional health. During young adulthood or middle age, most people with IED developed other mental disorders, usually depression, anxiety, or substance abuse."[6]

Steven Stosny, PhD, claims that,

> "The effects of anger on health have more to do with duration than frequency and intensity. The normal experience of overt anger lasts only a few minutes. But the subtle forms of anger, such as resentment, impatience, irritability, grouchiness, etc., can go on for hours and days at a time. Consistent, prolonged levels of anger give a person a five times greater chance of dying before the age of 50. Anger elevates blood pressure, increases threat of stroke,

heart disease, cancer, depression, anxiety disorders and, in general, depresses the immune system (angry people have lots of little aches and pains or get a lot of colds and bouts of flu or headaches or upset stomachs). To make matters worse, angry people tend to seek relief from the ill-moods caused by anger through other health-endangering habits, such as smoking and drinking, or through compulsive behaviour such as workaholism and perfectionism."[7]

Howard Martin of HeartMath Solution, an organisation promoting healthy hearts, said that, "We all know people who say: 'It's the principle of the matter' to justify sustaining toxic emotions for years. But as they hold onto their anger or hurt, they bleed away their energy reserves, often ending up bitter and depressed."

A casual search on Amazon.co.uk will produce more than 1,500 books on how to overcome or manage anger. With such a wealth of material available, why is it that our world still seems unable to come to terms with anger? One reason has to be the fact that most of these books will teach you to either "divert" or "redirect" your feelings of anger in an attempt to convert them into more positive emotions, or to let all your emotional rage out in an effort to "purge" yourself of the negative feelings. Arthur Janov, in particular, is a famous exponent of the latter method. Janov devised what has become known as "primal therapy" and published a book called *The Primal Scream* which advocated expressing long-repressed feelings of pain and anger in raw, emotional wails.

However, the uncontrolled release of anger will do you more harm than good. Anger is a destructive force that will hurt *you* more than it hurts anyone else, and it will have a serious impact on your health. The acting out of anger will only reinforce angry behaviour and it always fails to get to the root of the problem. Family sociologist Sue Meyers, writing here particularly about the effects of expressing anger on women, writes that,

> "Another study indicated that women who vented their anger were more pessimistic, lacked social support, sensed limited control over their lives, and had greater health problems. So venting anger can cause problems as well. It appears that neither venting nor suppressing anger benefits women. The source of anger for both is the inability to deal effectively with the situations which bring about the anger."[8]

Jack's story

The following true story provides an apt example of how anger operates. There was a man called Jack who was very happy in life. In fact, his happiness was the thing that most people noticed about him when they met him. He seemed to be so fulfilled and everyone believed his happiness was really genuine, because it was so infectious. And, why shouldn't he be happy? He had a good family: a lovely wife and two beautiful daughters who were at college. He owned a large house in the country. He was very active in his church. And he was the vice-president of a very large multinational corporation that paid him a six-figure salary.

I don't know whether there was a Job-like conversation going on behind the scenes of Jack's life, but one day the circumstances of his life began to turn. Without warning he was called into his boss' office and dismissed. He had been instrumental in building the company up, but now he was out on his ear. He had thought that financially he was set for life, but now the future looked very different.

All of this had a remarkable and instantaneous effect on Jack. His happiness vanished. His assured self-confidence was replaced with frustration. His friendly demeanour quickly turned to bitterness. His anger and emptiness were tangible. He even became suicidal.

The question I want to ask is this: what was going on in this man's life to so dramatically affect his disposition? In truth, this man's motivational values were completely off-centre. He had a kind of arrangement with God: "God, you look after me and I'll be happy. Give me a good wife, a good family, a good job and a good reputation and I will serve You with a smile. I will even pay my tithes."

But when all the material things he had were stripped away from him, Jack discovered that his trust was not in the Lord, but in his income, in his position. He had an idol in his life. When his goal of financial security was blocked he became an angry and frustrated man.

When God began to speak to Jack about this and he took an inventory of his life, he began to realise that he had been living very much for himself, though he looked like a model citizen to the outside world. Thankfully, he gave his heart back to Jesus and came to the point where he could say, "Lord, you take my life and make it what You want it to be." From that moment on his joy returned. Even though he now had "nothing" in comparison to what he had before, he discovered that the real purpose of life and living is to be with Jesus and that He alone can supply the needs of our lives.

Many of us live life like Jack. We are fine until tests and trials come, and when they do, we get angry and frustrated because they are blocking our goals.

Two types of anger

There are two major forms of anger. Firstly (as mentioned in the article on intermittent explosive disorder), there is *explosive* anger – anger that is directed outwards, and secondly, there is *implosive* anger – anger that is turned inwards. The second type is not always understood as anger. Some of the angriest people I know have never been known to raise their voice. We tend to think of anger as having a violent, outward expression: shouting, slamming doors, kicking the cat, etc. But anger can work either in that explosive expression or it can be something internal. Internally expressed anger usually breeds bitterness, resentment and malice, as Steven Stosny indicated.

These two forms of anger can sometimes be found together in the same person, but most people will tend towards one type or the other in an effort to deal with "goal blocking" circumstances in their lives. These types of anger can perhaps be best expressed visually – explosive anger being like a bomb that is about to detonate, and implosive anger like a boiling pot on the stove with its lid on. With the latter there is little visible sign of what is happening, but inside it is seething.

Are you the implosive or the explosive type? Either way we all need to learn to deal with our anger. Anger that is left unchecked or unresolved will fester and grow, and will adversely affect our attitudes, speech and behaviour towards others – especially the person, situation, organisation or institution that we judge to have caused us hurt or offence. Even those who never raise their voice, visibly lose their temper or express their anger physically, can reveal their anger through the language of criticism, judgementalism, coldness or withdrawal.

Anger: an inadequate expression of our needs

Marshall Rosenberg, a clinical psychologist and counsellor who specialises in conflict resolution, and who delivers many anger management seminars, was once invited into a high security prison wing to give a talk about how to deal with your anger to a number of prisoners who were "lifers" – mostly murderers. He talked about the negative effects of anger and reasoned with them that anger, when it is expressed, is a tragic miscommunication of our needs. Rosenberg put it to his audience that getting so angry with somebody that you would go so far as to kill them is a totally inadequate expression of our needs, because it is directed in completely the wrong direction. Punishing someone else for wronging you will never get your needs met.

Listening to Rosenberg was a mean-looking, muscle-bound prisoner who had so many tattoos that he looked like an oil painting. Taking everyone by surprise he suddenly began to cry and cry. No one could console him. The puzzled psychologist asked the man what was going on and he replied, "If only I had heard this before, I would never have killed that man." He had come to the realisation that the act of murder he had committed was due to nothing more than a boiling over of anger as an expression of an unmet need within him.

That's an extreme case, but perhaps you have people in your life who make you angry and who make you want to take inappropriate action against them? What about the person who irritates you in your workplace? Do you know anyone like that? The person who only has to walk into the room and say one thing and immediately your hackles are rising? In actual fact, that person irritates you because of something that is going on inside you. Maybe, because of their sarcastic comments, you feel they don't respect you and so your need for affirmation is not being met? That is likely to be the real heart of the problem. Will expressing your irritation through anger help that situation in any way? No! It will only make that person defensive, or perhaps more determined to rub you up the wrong way. Not only will expressing your frustration through anger not get your needs met, it is the very thing that will prevent you from fulfilling the purpose of God in your life. The Bible says that, "The wrath of man does not work the righteousness of God."

If you want to be angry...

Anger will quickly stifle your creativity and prevent you from functioning normally. There is a story about this happening to the great artist Leonardo Da Vinci. When he was painting the scene of the Last Supper, he had set aside a specific time when he would carry out the critical task of painting the face of Christ. Unfortunately, when the appointed time came he began the day by having a blazing row with one of his staff, which didn't end well. Every time he climbed up onto the scaffolding to paint the face of Christ, all he could think about was how angry he was with this person. Eventually he realised that there was no way he was going to be able to complete the painting until he got down off the ladder and went to the man and apologised.

Having done this he returned to his position and was able to complete the painting. There is nothing that will stop Christ being formed in you more than the uncontrolled expression of anger – whether it is the implosive or explosive kind.

The psychologist, Les Carter, wrote a book on anger in which he listed eleven things that, if you do them, are guaranteed to make you an angry person.[9] If you don't want to be angry then you must avoid doing the things that are on this list. I reproduce the list here, but with my own comments accompanying. I want us to think about what might be going on inside of people who act in these ways.

If you want to be angry, then...

1. *...Become a perfectionist.* If you want to be an angry person, then a good way to achieve it is to expect perfection of yourself and everyone else around you. If your goal is absolute perfection you are going to end up being a very frustrated person. What need is this type of person seeking to meet? Why would anyone want to live at that level of stress and pressure? Perhaps they believe that unless they attain a certain standard people are not going to like them or notice them? Remember the three basic motivational needs – security, significance and self-worth? Either of the latter two needs could be the result of perfectionism in a person's life. Perfectionists tend to feel that when everything is "up to scratch" they are in control of their circumstances and their environment, and they feel good because they feel they are someone who is having an impact on life. Right? Wrong! If you seek perfectionism,

sooner or later you will be angry, because perfection is an unachievable goal and inevitably results in frustration.

2. *... Don't listen to anyone else's view and keep pushing your own view.* Angry people are very often controlling people and it can apply to children as much as adults. Psychologists have identified a pattern of behaviour that has been termed "tyrannical child syndrome", when a child will suddenly turns into a "monster" in order to get his/her own way. Generally this type of behaviour begins at around two years of age, but equally, we all know some 22 year olds, or 32 year olds who practise a similar technique in order to get what they want. It is "the squeaky wheel gets the most oil" scenario. We learn that if we shout and scream loud enough we will get the attention we want. Often people will get what they want by exploding with anger and by punishing those around them, making them feel bad or guilty. Perhaps the need for this person is simply to be in control, to be acknowledged and recognised. Their outlook is: if you do things my way then I'm your friend; if you don't do it my way, then there's going to be trouble.

3. *... Overload your schedule.* If you make yourself so busy that you are always on the edge, overcommitted and stretched like a rubber band, then you will snap easily – usually at anyone who gets in the way and appears to be "ruining" your schedule. Why do people do that? Is it because they believe that the world can't do without them? Because they believe they are the only person who matters? Or is it because they believe that in order to be a person of significance it will be recognised through their achievements? We need to be set free from that mindset.

Our self-worth and significance can only be found in Christ and it is conferred on who we are, not on what we do.

4. *... Expect other people always to cater to your needs*. Angry people are often very selfish people and have a "me first" mentality. Anger in people like this tends to show up on their face first, because they are poor at communicating their needs. "What's wrong with you?" you may ask, puzzled by their moody expression. "I wanted to go to McDonalds," they seethe. "But, you're in Burger King," you offer. "Exactly!" they say. "Burger King is not McDonalds!" Always insisting on your personal preference and getting angry when you don't get exactly what you want will pitch you into battle with others on a daily basis. We need to learn to be at peace with one another and to respect one another's preferences. No one can expect to get their own way all the time.

5. *... Don't laugh a lot*. If you want to be an angry person then laughing a lot is prohibited. Some people take themselves so seriously that they believe their own publicity. Some angry people just need to lighten up a bit. They need to get a life!

6. *... Have no compassion for others*. Angry people tend to be inwardly focused, concerned that their needs are not being met and so have little time to think about the needs of others.

7. *... Put down other people*. It is so easy to judge others, perhaps because they come from a different culture or tradition. Angry people usually show disdain for others and especially sneer at anyone who is "different". Why is that? Because if you put other people down then it might make

you look a bit higher. Angry people often do not realise that, in fact, other people find their put-downs distasteful and inappropriate. The angry person feels superior when they are ridiculing others, but onlookers easily see through this type of behaviour. Paradoxically, angry people are at their angriest when *they* feel put down, so it becomes a matter of putting others down before they put you down.

8. ... *Shout at other people.* Why do people shout? Generally because they want to drown out other people's opinions and force their will on them. They do it because they want to intimidate, so that others will back down and let them have their way. Ambrose Bierce said, "Speak when you are angry and you will make the best speech you will ever regret"!

9. ... *Worship money and possessions.* In other words, put your faith in the wrong thing and you will be a very angry person. If you find your security by trusting in your financial investments then you will soon discover that your emotions rise and fall with the rate of exchange, with the interest rates, with the income tax rates! You will easily become frustrated, rather than fulfilled.

10. ... *Focus on the faults of others and learn to be easily offended by any remark.* If we focus on the faults of others and their weaknesses, instead of accepting that all of us (including you and me) make mistakes and are imperfect, then we will be constantly irritated. Angry people also tend to be easily offended. They are touchy and easily provoked to anger.

11. ... *Learn to nag, nitpick and criticise.* Angry people are often huge critics of others. Nothing is ever good

enough for them and they become troubled as soon as
something irritates them. Lacklustre service at a restaurant,
or someone pushing into a queue will be triggers for
them. Very often they will make their anger known
vocally.

In all of these examples, basic needs are not being met. Mostly,
angry people are suffering from a lack of affirmation regarding
their identity. Their feelings and emotions go up and down like a
rollercoaster depending on the perceived opinions of them held
by those around them. But there is a better way to live. We can
live with a no-blame mentality. There are many things in life
which we *could* blame if we wanted to; people do things wrong
all the time. But if we take that and apply it to our lives
personally and live with that level of blame we will cultivate a
blame mentality.

Angry people are so goal-driven that they often demand to be
in control and insist their view is accepted as "the right one".
They demand that people do things their way, all because they
can't cope with who they really are inside. They have to be
propped up by other people's actions and reactions. The answer
can only be to realise that Jesus is the only One able to satisfy
your needs and desires. No one else – either by coercion,
control, manipulation or domination – will be able to do that
for you, no matter how hard you try. It will never lead to the
satisfaction and fulfilment that only Jesus can bring.

Are you the implosive or explosive type? Use the following
exercise to help you to define whether you tend more towards
one or the other type of anger. Go through the check lists and
honestly assess how you deal with your anger.

Signs of implosive anger

Signs of anger turned inward are:

- Clamming up
- Refusing to communicate
- Shutting someone out or cutting them off
- Pretending nothing is wrong
- Hiding behind spiritual language
- Sugary sweet responses
- Ignoring someone
- Harbouring hurt feelings
- Vengeance, getting even
- Playing the victim, offended party or the martyr
- Brooding over the offence
- Self-pity
- Self-righteousness
- Keeping a record of sins
- Self-vindication
- Blame shifting
- Projecting your thoughts, actions or faults onto someone else
- Bearing grudge
- Spreading gossip and slander
- Blocking a person's blessing
- Working against someone
- Bearing malice
- Entertaining hateful thoughts and hard attitudes against the person
- Unforgiving and judgmental spirit
- Faultfinding

- Sarcasm
- Despising looks
- Rolling the eyes
- Put-downs
- Hostility

Signs of explosive anger

Signs of anger turned outward are:

- Blowing up
- Shouting
- Rage
- Mocking
- Facial expressions
- Physical gestures
- Losing your temper
- Angry, destructive words
- Swearing and cursing
- Abusive words
- Accusations
- Exaggerations
- Blaming
- Sarcasm
- Put downs
- Arguing
- Hateful talk
- Hurtful talk
- Fighting
- Physical violence
- Verbal violence

- Throwing things
- Retaliation
- Acts of revenge

How to deal with anger

The Bible says very plainly: *"Be angry, and do not sin"* (Psalm 4:4). The Bible acknowledges the fact that we will, at some point, be angry, but that we must not let that anger lead us down the path towards sinning. Whilst every person is different and the situations and circumstances which lead to the generation of anger in a person's emotions extremely diverse, there are guiding principles we can observe that will help us to deal with our anger. Here are seven steps that are roughly chronological:

1. Accept responsibility for your anger

We must realise that our anger is never the fault of others, even if they have sinned against you – which I know is really tough to accept because it goes against our natural tendencies. Others people's sin does hurt us, but their sin is ultimately their responsibility before God and not ours.

2. Deal with your anger in the right way

Don't let anger lead you down the negative path that brings hurt and destruction. That's what the Bible means when it says, "Be angry, and do not sin." It doesn't mean that it is OK to be angry in certain circumstances, as much as it means you will get angry at times, but don't let your anger lead you to sin. If your anger drives you act in a negative, destructive way, then obviously you are sinning. If your anger can be channelled in a positive way, i.e. you attack the problem and not the person, then you have dealt with it correctly.

The Greek word for anger, *orge*, is a word that suggests almost a natural force which rises within a person like sap rises in a tree in the spring time. It suggests a surge of emotion. If you catch that "surge" early enough, it is possible to prevent it from becoming destructive and redirect it in a positive way – towards solving whatever the problem that resulted in anger. In that way you can avoid sinning.

3. Deal with your anger immediately and don't let it fester

The Bible says, "Don't let the sun go down on your anger." Whenever I give premarital counselling to young couples I always impart this valuable advice: It is always best to deal with today's problems today and get the matter resolved. Never carry over anger into tomorrow. If it is not dealt with then it will turn to bitterness. I go as far as to say that if a problem cannot be resolved the same day and two more days go by, the couple should seek help from an impartial, mature Christian who can talk things over with them. If issues aren't dealt with there will come a time where there is so much baggage in a relationship that communication dries up. Very often, couples who seek counselling because of problems with their sexual relationship will have a lack of communication as their core problem. Both partners get into bed with so much baggage that intimacy is difficult!

4. Recognise the necessity for forgiveness and resolving of disagreements

When we have been hurt, our responsibility is to come before God, acknowledging that we have been hurt and to release forgiveness to the person involved. When we forgive people we must never pretend that we have not been hurt by their actions. The process of forgiveness, by definition, has to acknowledge there has been wrongdoing – that is how it starts. Often when someone apologises to us we say, "It doesn't matter." Well, of course, it *does* matter. When you apologise to someone else, don't let them get away with, "It doesn't matter." We should also work to resolve any differences of opinion that resulted in the friction in the first place. I can't deal with the issue of conflict resolution in detail here, but it is important to really listen to the other person's point of view, acknowledging their right to express a view, even if you happen to disagree with it. Using language that accurately describes your emotional needs, taking full ownership of them, and avoiding the language of blame are vital in diffusing such situations.

5. Control your anger and direct it towards the proper goal

Anger can be a powerful tool when it is directed towards a godly, rather than an ungodly end. Jesus channelled His anger at the misuse of the temple effectively in order to purge His Father's house. His anger was not uncontrolled, but focused towards a godly end – to cleanse the temple. Similarly, we must channel our negative emotions into solving the problem that is causing them, rather than heaping them upon others. Physical exercise can be a great asset in dispersing anger because it literally "burns off" the stress-inducing chemicals that are released into the body when we express anger. It also improves our mood because hard physical exercise stimulates the release of mood-regulating neurotransmitters in the brain, such as endorphins which cause feelings of wellbeing.[10]

6. Focus compassionately on the needs of others understanding why they do what they do

This is very helpful to do. It doesn't excuse the actions of others, but it helps a great deal in understanding their actions. It was Longfellow who said, "If we could read the secret history of our enemies, we should find in each man's life sorrow and suffering enough to disarm any hostility." Jesus adopted this approach when, on the cross, He said, "Forgive them Father, they don't know what they are doing." He showed compassion for His persecutors' sin and blindness. When we do the same it does not excuse anyone or indicate that what they have doing isn't wrong, but it does demonstrate a godly compassion. If we are only focused on the need of ours that is not being met, then we are not being compassionate towards the person who is offending us. When we understand what unmet needs they have, or what hurts they have suffered, we will better understand why they behave as they do.

Steven Stosny puts it this way: "Compassion for others is recognizing that their symptoms, defences and obnoxious behaviour come from a core hurt, validating it, and supporting them while they change it. Compassion does not excuse obnoxious behaviour. Rather, it keeps us from attacking the already wounded person, which allows focus on changing the undesired behaviour." [11]

7. Ask yourself what need of yours is behind your emotion of anger

This is so important. We need to frequently take a look at your own life and ask ourselves what we are depending on for our security. What are we hoping for to meet our needs? To get a certain job or to be in a certain profession? To achieve a certain standard of living? Where is our need for significance being met? What do we think will fill that need in us? If it is anything other than God and what He provides, we are setting ourselves up for an emotional disaster.

When we seek God to meet all our needs, however, we begin to see ourselves as God sees us. If we are continually seeking God for our needs we will find that we have the ability to forgive unreservedly and unconditionally when people sin against us and hurt us. We will be more inclined to seek reconciliation with others than to have a row and fall out with them. Rather than storing up malice in our heart, God will empower us to seek the wellbeing of others and to pray for those who seem to be intent on hurting us.

In the final chapter we will examine the effects of depression and loss of hope and learn how to combat them.

Depression and Loss of Hope

In Psalm 42 the psalmist expresses his heart to the Lord in the following moving dialogue:

> "As the deer pants for streams of water,
>   so I long for you, O God.
> I thirst for God, the living God.
>   When can I come and stand before him?
> Day and night, I have only tears for food,
>   while my enemies continually taunt me, saying,
>   'Where is this God of yours?'
>
> My heart is breaking
>   as I remember how it used to be:

I walked among the crowds of worshipers,
   leading a great procession to the house of God,
singing for joy and giving thanks –
   it was the sound of a great celebration!

Why am I discouraged?
   Why so sad?
I will put my hope in God!
   I will praise him again –
   my Savior and my God!

Now I am deeply discouraged,
   but I will remember your kindness –
from Mount Hermon, the source of the Jordan,
   from the land of Mount Mizar.
I hear the tumult of the raging seas
   as your waves and surging tides sweep over me.

Through each day the LORD pours his unfailing love upon me,
   and through each night I sing his songs,
   praying to God who gives me life.

'O God my rock,' I cry,
   'Why have you forsaken me?
Why must I wander in darkness,
   oppressed by my enemies?'
Their taunts pierce me like a fatal wound.
   They scoff, 'Where is this God of yours?'

Why am I discouraged?
   Why so sad?

> *I will put my hope in God!*
> *I will praise him again –*
> *my Savior and my God!"*   (Psalm 42 NLT)

The way in which we think about the world and perceive our life provide a filter through which we process everything that happens to us. This filter dictates the way in which we interpret the circumstances of our life which, in turn, dictates the emotions we experience. If we perceive that our present circumstances are meeting our needs, we feel happy. If we perceive they are not, we feel sad. For many, it is extremely disappointing when, like the psalmist, our circumstances in life don't match up to the way we would like them to be.

The psalmist perceives that somehow God has abandoned him because circumstances have turned against him. Of course, God has not and would never forsake him, but that is his perception at that moment. What should encourage us greatly about these verses is the fact that the psalmist can be brutally honest before God concerning his feelings and the struggles he is experiencing. God is never phased by this! Yet, for all that, he knows how to encourage himself in the Lord and keeps returning to this central truth: God is God and is worthy of our trust. The psalmist says unequivocally, "I *will* put my trust in God." That core truth forms a major part of our defense against depression and loss of hope as we will see throughout this chapter.

The root of depression and hopelessness

Sadness, depression and loss of hope all have the same root: an unrealisable goal. We have seen in previous chapters that fear is produced by an *uncertain* goal and anger is produced by a *blocked* goal. If we judge that, actually, it is *impossible* for us to achieve a particular goal – that we will never, ever reach it and our hopes and dreams have been dashed – then we will inevitably gravitate towards depression and hopelessness. Thank God that through His Son, Jesus, there can be deliverance from sadness, depression and loss of hope.

Although on first reading it is easy to think, "This isn't something that affects me", the fact is, everyone, at some time in their life, will experiences loss to one degree or another, and at that point we will be vulnerable to depression and hopelessness as something we hold dear is snatched away from us. There are various levels of loss we can experience:

- *Temporary.* Perhaps we injure ourselves in some way and for a while we are incapacitated which prevents us from doing the things we want to be doing. That kind of loss is temporary and we know it doesn't last forever. Shortly, we will recover and things will be back to normal. It can, however, result in a degree of depression. Perhaps, for example, because of a sporting injury we forfeit the one chance we had of playing for the first team etc.

- *Permanent.* There are others, however, who suffer permanent loss – for example, people who through an accident lose a limb and have to face the fact that life will never be the same again. Over time they have to learn to replace their loss with something else or adapt in some way to cope so that they can lead a relatively normal life. When you meet people who have a permanent disability, it is amazing how often they have conquered the negative circumstances of their life and can sometimes be the most cheerful and fulfilled of people. Why? Because they no longer look to their physical condition to give them value, meaning and purpose. The human spirit is stronger than the human body.

• **Deep loss**. But there is a loss that people experience that is deeper than either of the previous types. A loss so deep, fundamental and permanent to a person's sense of wellbeing that all hope in this area of their life is gone. Their loss is the realisation that a fundamental goal or need is *never* going to be met – not in the way they were hoping. People experience deep loss when they lose a close loved-one. Often, as well as grieving in a general sense, the person will feel deep regret for all the things they would have liked to have said to the deceased and will now be unable to.

The deep loss experience could, however, signal the beginning of an entirely new chapter in a person's life if it brings with it the realisation that we have been trusting in the wrong things instead of trusting solely in God. If we are trusting in people, things, situations and we lose all hope, then what we have lost is hope in the hopeless! We need to learn to continually place our confidence in the Rock, who is Jesus Christ – like the psalmist, who says to himself, "Why am I going around mourning and full of discouragement because of the oppression of my enemies? Soul, listen to me! You'd better start putting your hope in God, for I shall yet praise Him. He is my health and my countenance." Such a declaration is a strong, positive affirmation of our faith in God. It is a costly confession which goes way beyond simply saying: "Oh well, praise the Lord!" with a smile, even though you don't mean it. Such a confession is not putting your head in the sand or hiding your sorrow and suffering under a veneer of super-spirituality. Rather, it is a statement about the truth of the certainty of Jesus' accomplishment on the cross.

For many, retuning our minds so that we are completely reliant on God, rather than people, things, or circumstances, will require a major refocusing of our lives. We fall so easily into the trap of idolatry – trusting in something other than God. But this is one key to escaping the pull of depression and hopelessness. We must abandon all hope in the hopeless and put our trust in the God of all hope. Thank God if the hopeless fails us! It was never going to satisfy us anyway. All of our false foundations will be exposed and broken up when the storms of life hit us. Better that it happens now, sooner rather than later.

A broken spirit

The process of falling into depression can be traced to a loss of hope concerning a need of ours we perceive will never be met. This loss of hope triggers feelings of sadness and depression and causes a broken-heartedness that the Bible calls a "broken spirit". I know, from experience, that God understands this so much more than we will ever understand it ourselves.

Proverbs 18:14 says,

> *"The spirit of a man will sustain him in sickness,*
> *But who can bear a broken spirit?"*

I can think of people I have known who, although their body was wasting away, remained strong in their spirit. It is amazing and humbling to be in the presence of such people. Although the

outward man perishes, the inner man is being renewed day by
day by the Spirit of God. Even in the midst of sickness, disability,
pain and the adverse circumstances of life, there can be a
buoyancy in our spirit as the Holy Spirit sustains us. But who,
the Bible asks rhetorically, can bear a broken spirit, when all
hope is gone? One could have great health, a fat bank balance, a
marvellous house and a beautiful wife, but with a broken spirit,
none of these things would make any difference to us. True
spiritual contentment does not lie in any of these things.

Earlier, in chapter 17, the writer of Proverbs asserts that,

> *"A merry heart does good, like medicine,*
> *But a broken spirit dries the bones."*

(Proverbs 17:22)

In other words, if you are full of the Lord and happy and
rejoicing then your emotional and physical wellbeing will be
positively affected. But a broken spirit will rob you of your joy
and can lead to emotional and physical illness as the verse says.

The writer also says that,

> *"Hope deferred makes the heart sick,*
> *But when the desire comes, it is a tree of life."*

(Proverbs 13:12)

"Hope deferred" is the term the Bible uses to describe when all
our dreams, ambitions and desires lie in ruins. It produces a kind
of sickness in a person that is indescribable. This loss of hope can
trigger feelings of hopelessness and sadness, but it can also lead
to what is technically called depression (i.e. more than simply

feeling a bit down), whether it is mild, severe, acute, or even clinical depression requiring medical treatment.[12]

If you know anyone who is suffering from depression, please don't judge them. They may need encouragement, counselling and possibly prescriptive treatment from their doctor. As a temporary measure some treatments can help to balance the chemicals in the brain so that the person can begin to look at their life and face it positively.

Depression can be caused by several things besides a loss of hope:

- A physical condition – hormonal imbalances in the body
- It can be caused by a psychological condition – a mental illness
- It can have a spiritual cause – a spirit of depression or heaviness

But, it can be triggered by the circumstances of life we have already touched upon:

- Significant loss
- Trauma
- Change
- Deep disappointment

Your thoughts can determine your feelings including depression

I want now to return to the thought expressed at the beginning of this chapter – that our thought processes have much to do with the emotions we experience. It is an accepted principle of human psychology that our thoughts regarding our needs give rise to our emotions. This truth is consistent with the teaching of the Bible, although clinical psychologists would claim the principle as their own as expressed through the method of counselling known as Rational Emotive Therapy (RET). RET was developed by Albert Ellis, among others, who believed that your feelings don't control your thoughts – your thoughts control your feelings. Negative emotions, in this theory, are not inevitable, but come about as the result of patterns of thinking we have laid down over the years. If we can learn to rethink the situations we face in life, then we can learn to control negative emotions, so the theory goes. The Bible also makes the point that we need to think differently, but as ever, points to God as the answer. Scripture asserts that we need to have our minds renewed by focusing on and absorbing God's Word and so be transformed. Whilst we can tinker with manmade solutions like RET, God remains the best and most accomplished human psychologist.

The most crucial factor in all your experiences is how you choose to view your circumstances – because we *do* have a choice. How you view your circumstances is determined by the "grid" of your beliefs, values and thoughts, in particular where or how you think your needs will be met. Your unique worldview filter is like a pane of glass in front of you. If the grid is a good one you can see things clearly, but, if it is marked, tinted or spoiled in some way, then you will not see clearly. In particular, the grid through which we view the world will feed us vital information about whether or not we perceive certain situations are meeting our needs.

Depression and your needs

If you come to the point where you lose all hope of having your needs met, you will suffer from feelings of sadness and depression. But, it is possible to refocus and to look to Jesus and Him alone to meet your needs. He is never a disappointment and the Bible promises that whoever puts their trust in the Lord will never be ashamed.

Whenever we feel that we are tending towards depression, a little self-analysis is a helpful place to begin to solve the problem. We can ask ourselves, what do I believe I need to make me a happy, joyful and fulfilled person, so that if I had nothing else apart from this, I would still be satisfied? We know that the answer has to be Jesus! But, let's not jump in there right away. Most, if not all believers would immediately say, "The answer is Jesus", but the problem is that they don't live like He's the answer. They are still looking for the answer in relationships, finances, all kinds of experiences, positions (a career or perhaps ministry status), to give them their security, significance and self-worth. Their motivation towards those things and their passion in the pursuit of them is ten times more passionate than their pursuit of Jesus! God wants us to be passionate about Him.

I encourage you to do the following exercise by completing the following sentence:

In order for me to be fundamentally happy and fulfilled, I 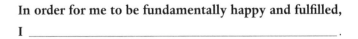 .

Please note: pat answers like "...I need to love Jesus more" are not allowed! This exercise aims to help you uncover what is really going on in your heart. How you live is a reflection of your motivational beliefs regarding your needs. If Christ is not absolutely 100% central in your life, then other things – that tantalising promotion to a new job, even though it might mean a bit of compromise, or that attractive girl who keeps catching your eye – will take precedence in your life and compromise your walk with God.

Years ago I knew the curate of a local Evangelical Anglican church near to where I lived. I got to know him fairly well and he was a lovely man. Being interested in the ministry I wanted to find out about how he ministered to people and I remember him saying, regarding depression, that, "The best way I have found of helping people to deal with it is telling them that you suffer from it yourself." He was sympathetic to what people were going through because he knew from experience what it was like. I guess, by his own admission, there was an area of depression in his life. But it wasn't long after that, sadly, that I discovered he had left his wife and run off with one of the other workers in the church. He committed adultery and then divorced and split the family.

As a young Christian that affected me. In my mind I was convinced that if you have Jesus in your life, then marriage should be "happily ever after". Well, it should be and it is if we abide in Jesus. But there was something in my friend's heart that was not centred on Christ. And from that day to this there are numerous cases of leaders across the world – godly, anointed men falling like flies in the battle. Immorality, sexual impurity, family break-up, financial impropriety, jealousy, criticism ... no one is immune. Just because we all know that the answer is Jesus, doesn't mean that any of us are going the way that He tells us.

It all comes down to how we fill out the blank in the core of our life. "In order for me to be fundamentally happy and fulfilled, I..." Whatever is slotted into the blank space at the end of that sentence is what we will really pursue in life. It will be what we dream about, what we long for, where our passion is. As Christians we are continually tempted to fill in the blank with something other than Christ. Ask yourself, where are your basic areas of temptation. What do I need to be careful of, so that Christ remains central in my life? What I dream about; what do I long for; where is my passion? Could you answer that question truthfully today? What would be some of the things the devil would tempt you with to say, "Do this because it will satisfy and fulfil you..." Where are your basic areas of temptation? Usually it revolves around the big three: money, sex and power. This is the reality of what is going on in our lives.

It is easy to see that the answer is "Jesus". Why then do so many believers enjoy such low levels of joy and satisfaction? Why do so many fall away from the Lord and go against His will in pursuit of satisfaction in things other than God? Because we are always tempted to pursue the things of the flesh to get what we want and because of our flawed thinking and sinful human nature we put our trust in the wrong things – people, situations or circumstances we hope will meet our needs.

A person might fill in the blank in this sentence with the following things, each of which sounds perfectly legitimate at a glance:

- ...I need to be married
- ...I want healthy children

- ... I want to be pain free
- ... I need to be recognised by my peers
- ... I want to be a person of significance in the eyes of others
- ... I need to have a successful career
- ... I want to have a lot of money

Most people have very simple ideas regarding what will make them happy; they don't necessarily have a huge, unrealistic wish list. Most people just want simple, basic things, but happiness is very elusive. Happiness is not an end in itself that we can seek out and grasp hold of, because it is a by-product of seeking God and putting His kingdom first. Jesus said,

> *"Blessed are those who hunger and thirst for righteousness,*
>   *For they shall be filled."*

(Matthew 5:6)

What then prevents us from coming alive with passion for the things of God, so that we would know the true happiness only He can give us? The answer is our negative thinking.

The place negative thinking has in negative emotions

Most believers don't truly believe that righteousness equals satisfaction and happiness. If they did they would be pursuing it with all their might! Our negative, skewed thinking about what we need to be fulfilled continually leads us down rabbit trails that are heading in the wrong direction.

Negative thinking has a huge role to play in our emotions. If you think negative and talk negative, you become negative. Negative feelings follow on from our negative thoughts and negative feelings will feed our negative thought processes, establishing a vicious cycle which can easily spiral out of control.

In addition, we often wrongly communicate our feelings by using confusing language and muddling up our evaluations/ perceptions of a situation with our emotional responses. We begin mixing up our thoughts, feelings and intentions and say "I feel..." a lot, putting wrong labels on our needs and emotions. For example, "I feel...

* ...unworthy."
* ...unloved."
* ...useless."
* ...valueless."
* ...taken for granted."
* ...rejected."
* ...abandoned."
* ...hopeless."

None of these statements describe feelings. They are not emotions, they are judgements, evaluations and interpretations based on how we view the things that are happening to us. "Unworthy" is not a feeling. We judge ourselves to be unworthy in our own eyes or in other's eyes and that generates negative emotions. In effect we program ourselves to believe that our need for self-worth will not be met by our present circumstances. What is needed in such a situation is for us to change our judgement of ourselves and to understand how God views us. If we grasped just how much Jesus loves us and values us, all our unworthiness would be lost forever is an ocean of His worthiness and passion for us! Once we realise this, we will begin to feel completely different about ourselves. This is why it is so vital to deal with our flawed thinking.

You may say, "I feel rejected and abandoned." For those suffering from depression and loss of hope, it can be one of the loneliest experiences, because you feel that nobody is for you – you feel completely alone. But the truth is that "alone" is not a feeling, it is a judgement. It is an assessment because the significant "others" in your life have failed to meet your needs in the way they should – but, the truth is they can never meet that need in you. There is a God-shaped void in you that only Jesus can fill. "Rejected" and "abandoned" are evaluations; they are your interpretation of your circumstances.

Hope for the future

So, what is the solution to depression and hopelessness? To put your hope in the Lord. If depression comes when we see that our goals will never be met – i.e. we have no hope – then to hope in Christ is to see that there is hope for all our needs in the future. Hope always has to do with the future; it is not about today. The Bible says that if we put our trust, our hope, in Jesus, He promises to meet all our needs. We can know that our future wellbeing is assured, because God has promised it.

Each person who comes to Christ and believes in Him is saved, but saved "in hope" because salvation is an ongoing process. We are saved, we are being saved, and we will be saved. If something is fully in your possession then you don't have to hope for it. So, although we have received salvation, there is much more to come! The hope of the resurrection; the hope of our future with Christ in heaven; the hope of fulfilment and reward...

And so the psalmist says,

> *"Why are you cast down, O my soul?*
> *And why are you disquieted within me?*
> *Hope in God;*
> *For I shall yet praise Him,*
> *The help of my countenance and my God."*

(Psalm 42:11)

Remember, God has a future and a hope for you...

> *"For I know the thoughts that I think toward you, says the* LORD, *thoughts of peace and not of evil, to give you a future and a hope."*

(Jeremiah 29:11)

As we "hope in the Lord" we are trusting that this statement is true. We are building on the foundation that the future God has for us is the total fulfilment of all our needs. We may need to persevere and to learn patience along the way; there may be some suffering and pain; but God will never forsake us and He *will* meet all our needs. And I'm not just talking about the afterlife! God has not said to us, "You will be with me in heaven and enjoy bliss for eternity, but while you are on earth you will be miserable!" (though even if that were the case it would be a pretty good deal. Who would not endure about 70 years of misery for the promise of an eternity of joy?).

We know that not everything in life will always go our way, but the important thing is for us to keep persevering as James points out:

> *"My brethren, take the prophets, who spoke in the name of the Lord, as an example of suffering and patience. Indeed we count them blessed who endure. You have heard of the perseverance of Job and seen the end intended by the Lord – that the Lord is very compassionate and merciful."*

(James 5:10–11)

What that means is, despite your present circumstances, God is faithful and our hope in Him is not unfounded. Though we may at times struggle to understand the circumstances we are living through, God never abandons us and He always works for the good of those who love Him. Even though your dreams seem to be crumbling around you, God is so faithful, merciful and compassionate. Our own precious daughter, Laura, contracted a viral meningitis when she was very small which destroyed her brain and she lived on this earth for sixteen years under the twenty-four hour supervision of my wife, Amanda. We both prayed and believed and even saw visions of healing for her, but it was not to be. We know that Laura is healed now and in heaven with Jesus, for which we are very grateful. It is not the future that we dreamed would happen. We looked for life on earth; we looked for that elusive happiness, but God gave us something else – something extraordinary. Our hope is not in our circumstances. Our hope is in the Lord.

I have heard reports that some people stopped going to

church because of the Asian tsunami. We frequently hear reports of suffering from all around the world. But if we lose loved ones, or our dreams are shattered, that is not a reason to reject God – it is a reason to love Him all the more, because He is there when you need Him, when you are desperate and down; He will comfort the comfortless.

Our suffering provides a greater reason than ever to believe in God. Not because we need a crutch, but because we understand what life is all about and it is not about present comfort and fulfilment as much as it is about spending eternity in God's presence. I would rather have my relationship with Jesus and fullness in Him than all of the other things that the world pretends to be able to give to us.

Finding hope again

Here are a number of exercises on hope that will help those who are feeling depressed or hopeless. Even if you are not feeling depressed, it will be an uplifting experience to work through the Bible verse and to realise afresh the depth and intensity of God's love for you, and His commitment to your wellbeing.

Throughout the Bible God consistently speaks hope to His people, no matter how dire the circumstances. He has never changed and wants to do the same for us today. He does this so we can learn that when things are at their bleakest, He is there for us, our comfort, our strength, reassuring us that the hard times will pass and our future in Him is glorious. Meditate on the following Bible verses and write down how they relate to you and your personal circumstances:

- *"For I know the thoughts that I think toward you, says the LORD, thoughts of peace and not of evil, to give you a future and a hope"* (Jeremiah 29:11).

  _____

  _____

  _____

  _____

- *"Be of good courage, and He shall strengthen your heart, all you who hope in the LORD"* (Psalm 31:24).

  _____

  _____

  _____

  _____

- *"Why are you cast down, O my soul? And why are you disquieted within me? Hope in God, for I shall yet praise Him for the help of His countenance"* (Psalm 42:5).

  _____

  _____

  _____

  _____

- *"For You are my hope, O Lord GOD; You are my trust from my youth. By You I have been upheld from birth; You are He who took me out of my mother's womb. My praise shall be continually of You. I have become as a wonder to many, but You are my strong refuge. Let my mouth be filled with Your praise and with Your glory all the day"* (Psalm 71:5–8).

  _____

  _____

  _____

  _____

• *"But I will hope continually, and will praise You yet more and more"* (Psalm 71:14).

_____

_____

_____

_____

• *"Therefore, having been justified by faith, we have peace with God through our Lord Jesus Christ, through whom also we have access by faith into this grace in which we stand, and rejoice in hope of the glory of God. And not only that, but we also glory in tribulations, knowing that tribulation produces perseverance; and perseverance, character; and character, hope. Now hope does not disappoint, because the love of God has been poured out in our hearts by the Holy Spirit who was given to us"* (Romans 5:1–5).

_____

_____

_____

_____

• *"For we were saved in this hope, but hope that is seen is not hope; for why does one still hope for what he sees? But if we hope for what we do not see, we eagerly wait for it with perseverance"* (Romans 8:24–25).

_____

_____

_____

_____

- *"Now may the God of hope fill you with all joy and peace in believing, that you may abound in hope by the power of the Holy Spirit"* (Romans 15:13).

  _____

  _____

  _____

  _____

- *"For the grace of God that brings salvation has appeared to all men, teaching us that, denying ungodliness and worldly lusts, we should live soberly, righteously, and godly in the present age, looking for the blessed hope and glorious appearing of our great God and Saviour Jesus Christ"* (Titus 2:11–14).

  _____

  _____

  _____

  _____

Dealing with wrong thinking

As mentioned at the beginning of this chapter, our negative emotions are chiefly generated by negative thinking. The following exercises are designed to help you bring your thought life into alignment with the Word of God by identifying and eliminating ungodly, negative thoughts and beliefs.

1. Identify and replace the messages of hopelessness and negativity you are repeating to yourself, such as:

- Hopelessness – "What's the use of trying – it never works."
- Alienation – "I am all alone – no one really cares."

- Rejection – "I'm not wanted."
- Powerlessness – "There's nothing I can do."
- Worthlessness – "I'm useless."

These are the kind of messages you must learn to change. Start working on this now by listing some of the specific messages you personally have "played" to yourself over and over again, and alongside them the new messages you are going to repeat to yourself which reflect the truth about you in Christ:

- **I must replace the following negative false messages:**

_____

_____

_____

_____

_____

_____

_____

_____

- **With these messages of truth and hope:**

_____

_____

_____

_____

_____

_____

_____

_____

2. Identify the need at the root of your feelings of despair

What need of yours is not being met to the point that you are beginning to wonder if it will ever be met? You can find the answer to this question by looking at the things that have brought you disappointment in life and then tracing these back to the needs you were hoping these things might meet in you.

So, for example, if you are feeling depressed because you haven't found your life partner, understand that your feelings of sadness or depression are not caused by these circumstances. Rather, they come from the mistaken belief that you need to be married and to have a family in order to be happy. Understand that only God can fulfil your deepest needs for companionship and relationship.

List your disappointments:

- **"I am disappointed in life because . . . "**

  _____

  _____

  _____

  _____

  _____

Now identify the *real* need at the root of these disappointments revealing the false belief that is at the root of your struggle with the negative emotions related to a loss of hope in these areas:

- **"I recognise that I have been looking for my need of . . . "**

  _____

  _____

- ...to be met by the following people, conditions and circumstances of life:"

_____

_____

_____

_____

_____

_____

_____

_____

_____

_____

_____

_____

3. Recognise that these needs can only be met by God and begin to redirect the passions of your heart towards the Lord and pursue Him to fulfil these needs in you directly

Record the practical changes this will mean for your life:

- **Instead of looking for my need of** _____
  to be met by _____
  I will now pursue the Lord for the satisfaction and fulfilment He alone can bring by seeking Him in the following ways:

_____

_____

_____

_____

_____

_____

- **Practically, this means . . .**

(List the practical changes this will mean for you by showing what you would have done when faced with certain situations and how you will now handle those same circumstances.)

When faced with _____

Before I would:	*But now I will:*
1. _____	_____
_____	_____
_____	_____
2. _____	_____
_____	_____
_____	_____
3. _____	_____
_____	_____
_____	_____
4. _____	_____
_____	_____
_____	_____

4. Commit your life into His hands on a daily basis trusting Him to direct your life into His will and fulfilment in all these areas

> "My son, do not forget my law, but let your heart keep my commands; for length of days and long life and peace they will add to you. Let not mercy and truth forsake you; bind them around your neck, write them on the tablet of your heart, and so find favour and high esteem in the sight of God and man. Trust in the LORD with all your heart, and lean not on your own understanding; in all your ways acknowledge Him, and He shall direct your paths." (Proverbs 3:1–6).

- **After 3 weeks of practising these principles, what differences can you see in your life?**

_____

_____

_____

_____

_____

_____

_____

_____

_____

_____

My prayer and belief is that you will have seen a marked difference in your moods and demeanour after exposing the ungodly beliefs you previously held and focusing upon the truth of God's Word regarding your true value, worth, and the future that God holds in His hands for you.

Conclusion

Throughout this book I have sought to help you to take control of your emotions, rather than letting your emotions take control of you. My prayer is that the reader will appreciate what constitutes a truly biblical balance regarding emotional expression and wellbeing. Our emotions should never be pushed down or ignored, but neither should they rule and run our lives so that we feel out of control. God has given us our emotions to add a richness, depth and colour to our lives. Without them, life would be a dull, grey, clinical experience.

Above all, the thought I want to leave with you is the one that has been stressed throughout this book – our emotions are stimulated by our needs and our needs can only be met in Christ. If you make a decision to seek God and His kingdom as your number one priority, then emotional wellbeing and wholeness will follow.

Colin Dye
August, 2006

Appendix: Emotional Problems and Mental Health

Notes to those who counsel others

In life and ministry we have to recognise and accept that some of the challenges people face are very serious ones. In many situations individuals who come for counselling (and indeed we may recognise this in ourselves) may be suffering from mental health problems and need medical attention. Prayer and scriptural verses alone will not be enough. If they are suffering from acute anxiety or depression, usually they are unable to concentrate sufficiently to read the Bible or pray and they need to be referred to a doctor or hospital. As cell members, leaders or counsellors we should not feel we have failed them if we refer people with such needs to medical professionals. We can go on supporting them and praying for them alongside their medical care or treatment.

Some of the challenges, which come up in counselling, could be extreme fear or anxiety; they usually go hand in hand – fear producing worry and worry producing anxiety which can also develop into depression.

Anxiety

Anxiety is a symptom, a response to a potentially challenging or threatening experience. When the threat is not acute or sudden and we have to think about it beforehand, worry and nervousness can produce anxiety. Anxiety is closely linked to fear which is a primary emotion that helps us deal with danger.

Not all anxiety is negative. It can be very positive. Some form of anxiety is unavoidable in our present hectic society and it is the body's way of telling us to pay attention, especially in dangerous situations, otherwise the consequences could be disastrous. But sometimes, anxiety seems to spiral out of control and it becomes a serious issue which begins to take over a person's life. Desperate feelings of anxiety, which are not related to obvious external circumstances, seem to dominate a person's thoughts. They are filled with a sense of dread and negative foreboding. Severe problems of anxiety like this, which can often be linked to depression, need medical input.

Depression

There are many different forms of depression – from discouragement to severe depression and everything in between. Life issues often get people down and usually ministry and support will bring this individual back to a place of trust and confidence in God to bring them through. But a person who has prolonged sadness with unrelenting symptoms becomes unable to enjoy life and loses interest in everything. This results in a pervading sense of hopelessness, feelings of dread and a general lack of ability to concentrate or to control thoughts. This is a disabling condition and needs urgent medical help.

People suffering from depression will usually have a chemical imbalance in their body, which is why they are prescribed some form of medication. When that is corrected they can enter fully into the counselling process.

For Christians to accept they are depressed can be very difficult and so they need a lot of encouragement and support to seek medical attention and indeed to take the medication prescribed (if there is a prescription).

In John 5:2–9, we read the story of the man by the pool with no one to put him in when the waters were troubled. When Jesus came along he was totally healed. There is emotional healing as well as physical healing in the cross. Healing is available for fear, rejection, poor self-image, past hurts and every other symptom of damaged emotions. When we release forgiveness to the individuals who have hurt us we step into the pool. And that pool is big enough for all of us.

Notes

1. Dorothy L. Law, *Children Learn What They Live* (published 1 April, 1959, in Torrance Schools Board of Education newsletter and later revised and published in the book *Children Learn What They Live*, Workman Publishing Co., New York, 1998).
2. Research by the Australian Drug Foundation showed that, "though marijuana is not necessarily a direct cause of mental disorders, there is considerable evidence to suggest it can bring them to the surface." *Source*: www.opendoors.com.au. An article in *The Lancet* in 2004 identified associations between cannabis use and psychological health problems in young people (*The Lancet*, Vol. 363, 15 May, 2004).
3. Taken from: *The Counsellor's Handbook* (various authors) Stanley Thornes, STP, pp. 64–65.
4. *Nature's Law* by Embrace, © 2006, Independiente Ltd.
5. Mentioned in an article by Dr Jack Singer, a practising Industrial/ Organisational Consultant based in California, recognised as a leading North American expert in organisational training.
6. Article by Bruce Bower entitled, "All the Rage: Survey extends research of explosive anger disorder". www.sciencenews.org/ articles/20060610/fob4.asp
7. Article entitled, "Anger and Health", 2004. http://mensightmagazine.com/Articles/Stosny/angerhealth.htm
8. Adapted from "How anger affects your health" in University of California, *Berkeley Wellness Letter*, Volume 8, Issue 4, January 1992.
9. Les Carter, *The Anger Trap: Free Yourself From the Frustrations That Sabotage Your Life*, Jossey Bass Wiley, 2003. See also, *Getting the Best of Your Anger*, Revell, 1997.
10. Anger is a trigger for the body's fight or flight response. The adrenal glands flood the body with stress hormones such as adrenaline or cortisol. Numerous studies have identified that regular exercise can improve mood and reduce stress levels.
11. Ibid.
12. See notes on depression in the Appendix.

We hope you enjoyed reading this New Wine book.
For details of other New Wine books
and a range of 2,000 titles from other
Word and Spirit publishers visit our website:
www.newwineministries.co.uk